Come and See

THE LIFE OF MARY BAKER EDDY

UNITED STATES

❧ THE UNION IN 1861 ❧

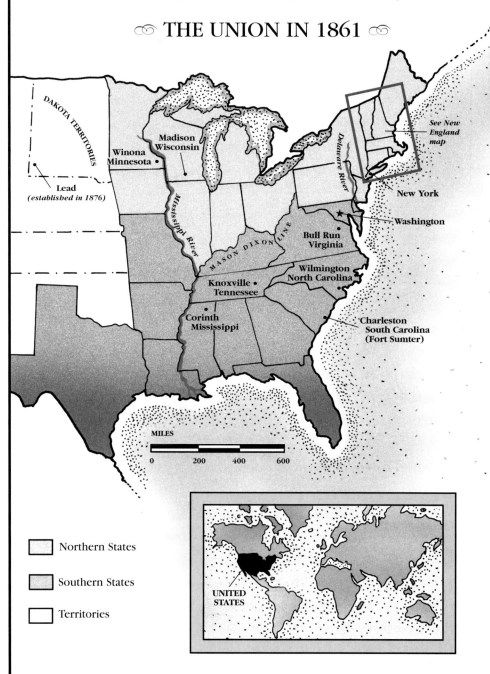

DAKOTA TERRITORIES

Lead
(established in 1876)

Winona
Minnesota

Madison
Wisconsin

Mississippi River

MASON DIXON LINE

Delaware River

See New
England
map

New York

Washington

Bull Run
Virginia

Wilmington
North Carolina

Knoxville
Tennessee

Corinth
Mississippi

Charleston
South Carolina
(Fort Sumter)

MILES

0   200   400   600

UNITED
STATES

Northern States

Southern States

Territories

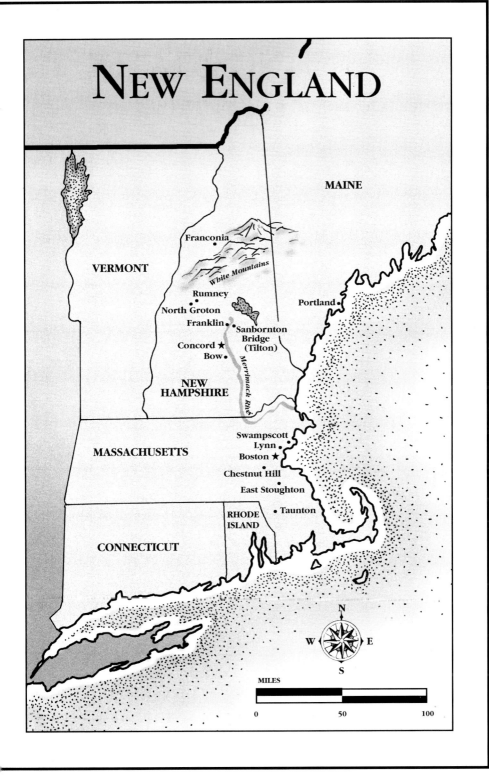

NEW ENGLAND

MAINE

VERMONT

Franconia

White Mountains

Rumney

North Groton

Franklin

Sanbornton
Bridge
(Tilton)

Concord ★

Bow

Portland

NEW
HAMPSHIRE

Merrimack River

MASSACHUSETTS

Swampscott

Lynn

Boston ★

Chestnut Hill

East Stoughton

Taunton

RHODE
ISLAND

CONNECTICUT

N

W   E

S

MILES

0   50   100

Come and See

THE LIFE OF MARY BAKER EDDY

—m—

by Isabel Ferguson

with illustrations by Joan Wolcott

Small Rain Press

Published by Small Rain Press
Box 400, Lincoln, Massachusetts 01773
www.smallrainpress.com

Cover design, book design and maps
by C. Porter Designs

Cover picture credits:
Photograph courtesy of The First Church of Christ,
Scientist, and The Mary Baker Eddy Library for the
Betterment of Humanity, Inc. Detail of manuscript
page © 2001 The Writings of Mary Baker Eddy.
All rights reserved.

Text copyright © 2001 by Isabel Ferguson
Illustrations copyright © 2001 by Joan Wolcott
All rights reserved.

First printing 2001

Printed in the United States of America

Every effort has been made to attribute ownership
of the art used in this book and to honor verbal and
written agreements for its use. Errors made are inad-
vertent and, if brought to the attention of Small Rain
Press, they will be corrected in future printings.

Publisher's Cataloging-in-Publication
(Provided by Quality Books, Inc.)

Ferguson, Isabel.
    Come and see : the life of Mary Baker Eddy / by
Isabel Ferguson. -- 1st ed.
        p. cm.
    Includes bibliographical references and index.
    SUMMARY: Warm telling of the biography of Mary Baker
Eddy, a healer and the woman who founded Christian
Science.
    Audience: 5th grade on up.
    LCCN 2001132906
    ISBN 0-9655317-3-2 (HC)
    ISBN 0-9655317-2-4 (PB)

    1. Eddy, Mary Baker, 1821-1910--Juvenile literature.
2. Christian Scientists--United States--Biography--
Juvenile literature. [1. Eddy, Mary Baker, 1821-1910.
2. Christian Scientists. 3. Women--Biography.] I.
Title.

BX6995.F47 2001   289.5'092
                         QBI01-700816

To you, who read this book
with an open mind

—◊◊◊—

Special Thanks to

Joan Wolcott, who not only graces this book with
her illustrations, but has been its chief
supporter, critic and consultant.

Jacqueline Dembar Greene, well-known children's
author, who urged me to write from inside
the main character.

Cheryl Moneyhun, Assistant Director, Museum
Collections, Longyear Museum, who provided
invaluable assistance in my research, and
with the selection of visual materials.

And to Joseph Ferguson, my patient husband.

I would also like to thank the archivists and
reference librarians who helped make this book
more accurate, notably those at Old Sturbridge
Village, the Lynn Museum and the Weston
Public Library. These resourceful
people know how and where
to look things up!

TABLE OF CONTENTS

Come and See

THE LIFE OF MARY BAKER EDDY

CHAPTER ONE

The Voice

"Mary."

The call was low and distant.

"Mary."

It came again, still gentle, but firm — and louder.

"MARY!" Now the voice seemed very close.

Mary, who was eight, pretended not to notice. She bent her curly, brown head and shifted her little chair closer to her twenty-three-year-old cousin, Mehitable, who was visiting the family that day. Mehitable looked up, as though she heard something, but Grandmother calmly continued with her knitting.

Mary wished the call would go away. She had been hearing it off and on for almost a year. It sounded like her mother's voice, but when she ran to her, Mrs. Baker would shake her head. No, she had not called.

"Mother, who *did* call me? I heard somebody call *Mary* three times!" This had happened so often that Mary felt discouraged, and her mother perplexed and worried.

Again the call came, three times in an ascending scale.

"Why don't you go? Your mother's calling you!" Mehitable spoke sharply.

Mary got up, hoping her cousin was right, and ran to the kitchen.

"What is it, Mother?"

"Nothing, child!" Mrs. Baker's plump, cheerful face had a puzzled frown.

Mary persisted. "Mehitable heard you calling, too."

Mrs. Baker dried her hands and led the way back to Grandmother's room. She took the older girl into the next room, but left the door open. Mary moved closer. She could hear her mother. "Almost a year now...mysterious voice." And then, "Did you really hear Mary's name being called?" Mary caught her breath.

"Yes," Mehitable answered quickly.

Mary let out a deep sigh. This was the first time someone else had heard the voice. No one had believed her before. That night, before Mary's mother tucked her into bed, she read her the Bible story of little Samuel, who also heard a voice calling his name.

"When the voice comes again, Mary, answer the way Samuel did: 'Speak, Lord; for thy servant heareth.'" Her mother was smiling, but her eyes were serious. Mary's chest tightened. Could she really answer all by herself?

Mary was alone when the voice came again. She felt afraid and could not speak.

"Sorry, God," she said later, as tears wet her cheeks. "Please forgive me."

Next time, she told herself, I will do what Mother says. When the call came again, she did answer. "Speak, Lord; for thy servant heareth," but never again was that mysterious call repeated.

Mary had three older brothers, Samuel, Albert, and George, and two older sisters, Abigail and Martha. When Mary was eight, Samuel, then twenty-one, had already left home for Boston, Massachusetts, to learn the building trade. Albert, her favorite second brother, who read to her when she was sick, had gone off to college. Only George, her impulsive third brother, was left at home to work on the farm and to laugh with his three younger sisters as they played around the kitchen table after supper. Abigail, called Abi by the family, was fourteen. She wanted to be a grand lady, and liked to order the two younger girls about. Martha, eleven, was good at telling stories and writing letters.

Mary often read the Bible by herself. It was one of her favorite books. Sometimes when Martha and Abi went out to play, she would stay at home reading, or pull up her rocking chair close to her grandmother. Grandmother Baker came from Scotland. Her family had been Covenanters, strong and daring characters who had fought for religious freedom. Among her treasures was a heavy sword in a brass scabbard that had been given to a kinsman by Sir William Wallace. Mary liked to grasp the round pommel while Grandmother sang her the rousing song, "Scots wha hae wi' Wallace bled."

Mary was very careful when Grandmother let her open some of her special books printed in old type, or read her newspapers, yellow with age. She also told the young girl about the American side of her family — General Henry Knox, who fought in the Revolutionary War, and Captain John Lovewell of Dunstable, New Hampshire. He was a gallant leader who died in the Indian wars in the 1720's. For his brave service, he was given a grant of land, the same land which they farmed and where their house now stood.

Captain Lovewell's daughter, Hannah, was Mary's great-grandmother, a woman of courage. One time when Hannah Lovewell Baker was out washing clothes by a spring, she heard the alarm — Indians coming! While everyone ran to the nearest garrison

house, Hannah finished her laundry. When a rescue party went out to save her, they found Hannah calmly walking to the fort, her basket of clean clothes on her hip. From these stories Mary learned that her family were fighters who did not easily give up.

Grandmother also told Mary about clearing the land and building the farmhouse in Bow, New Hampshire, where they lived. The house and two barns stood on the rise of a hill. If Mary looked out on one side, she saw the fields where in summer the wind whispered through the tall grain. Beyond lay the smooth, glassy face of the Merrimack River, with its canal boats laden with freight. If Mary ran out to a rocky ledge on the lower part of the hill, she came to "the playground" and could look down on the turnpike, where stagecoaches swirled by on their way to nearby Concord, the capital of New Hampshire, or faraway Boston.

Mary felt closest to her mother. She followed her around the house and helped in the kitchen. Her mother taught her not to waste anything. One time when they were picking out dried corn for the chickens, a kernel rolled out of Mary's fingers onto the floor. She started pushing it with her foot toward the open fire.

"Mary, get down and pick up that corn," her mom quickly said.

"Oh! Mother, it's only one grain."

"Never mind, it will help make a meal for a little chick."

As Mary bent down, she thought of the peeping, fluffy chicks. If one looked weak or sickly, she put it inside the front of her dress to keep it warm and quiet. Then, when it felt better and its little legs scratched against her, she reached in and set the feathery bundle gently on the ground. Off it scooted to its mother, who was clucking to her brood and pecking the dirt for good things to eat.

Mary loved all of the farm animals — the strong, solid oxen used for the heavy work, with their shiny, wet noses and dainty hoofed feet; the horses that pulled the wagon; the cows, sheep, and pigs. When the little pigs squealed too loudly at 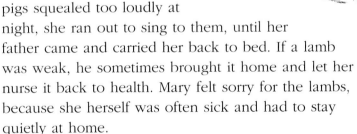 night, she ran out to sing to them, until her father came and carried her back to bed. If a lamb was weak, he sometimes brought it home and let her nurse it back to health. Mary felt sorry for the lambs, because she herself was often sick and had to stay quietly at home.

When she felt well, Mary walked with Abi and Martha to School #3 at the crossroads a mile away. They went in the summer, when school was less crowded as the older boys were out working in the fields. On her first day Mary followed her sisters down the hill, through the orchard and neighbor Gault's woods, and into the schoolhouse. The teacher was waiting for them at her raised desk. Mary, who was born on July 16, 1821, was almost five. She sat on a bench in the front row. She had never been with so many children before. All eight grades were together in one room.

Abi and Martha could hardly wait until lunch, when they could run over and talk to their little sister. They sat her on a table while the others crowded around.

"What do you want to do when you grow up, Mary?" someone asked. Most of the girls wanted to be mothers or teachers. The boys thought of being farmers like their dads.

"I want to write a book," she answered, and everybody laughed.

When Mary could not go to school she studied her lessons at home. Albert, her favorite brother, helped her when he came back from his studies for the summer. He wanted her to learn something new each day, so he taught her a little of what he was studying — Latin, Greek, and Hebrew. He also encouraged her to read Shakespeare and to write poetry. In the fall of 1829 Mary was especially glad, because Albert became the teacher at School # 3 and could help her during the winter months.

Mary looked up to her tall, handsome brother, with his dark auburn hair and clear brown eyes full of intelligence and love. Albert believed that people make mistakes because they do not know any better. If they knew not to lie or cheat or steal, that would free them to be honest and true. He wanted people to hurry up and learn, not only things like science and math, or art and music, but also right from wrong.

Albert graduated from Dartmouth College with honors. Soon afterward, General Benjamin Pierce and his wife invited the young man to come and live with them in their fine house in Hillsborough while he studied law with their son, Franklin. The Pierces were old

family friends, the General often stopping at the Baker house when he visited Bow. Their son, Franklin, who was a successful young lawyer, later invited Albert to join his law practice.

Besides the Pierces, Mary saw many visitors coming to the house. "My childhood's home, I remember as one with the open hand," she later wrote. Her parents often shared meals with people who were poor and, like many other families in the community, the Bakers especially welcomed ministers from the church. Mr. Baker liked nothing better than to argue over strongly held religious beliefs or the meaning of a Bible verse with his friends. Mary would lie awake in bed, listening to the rise and fall of their voices, following each point, waiting for hours to hear who had won. One time when Mary was twelve, she herself got into a fierce argument with her father.

CHAPTER TWO

What's Right?

Mary's father, Mark Baker, was a man of strong character and highly respected in the community. He was a clear and forcible speaker whose opinion was valued, and who was often asked to help settle neighbors' disputes. He was a justice of the peace, served on the school committee, and was clerk of the Congregational Church. He treated all men with kindness and respect, and was known to be generous and fair.

"At Christmastime," Mary told a friend, "father would fill the democrat wagon with turkeys, chickens, and vegetables and go with them to the poor of the neighborhood. Every present was nicely done up and there was something for every needy neighbor."

Although he was the youngest of nine children, Mark had inherited the family home and, with his older brother, James, about five hundred acres of land. A hundred acres or so were cultivated — fields of grain, green pastures bright with wildflowers, orchards of apples, peaches, pears, and cherries.

Each morning, Mary saw her father get up early to tend to the animals and work on the land. He could turn his hand to many things, even making shoes for a family in need. But she knew that he preferred to go off to court to argue for his neighbors when they faced a legal battle. She also saw how much time and energy he spent in helping run the school, the town, and the church. Mark became clerk of the Congregational Church in Bow the year after Mary was born. In clear, precise handwriting he wrote in the church record book, "...it is the duty of heads of families to train up the children under their care for GOD, by all good precepts and examples and by praying with and for them night and morning."

Morning and evening Mark read to his family a chapter from the great old Bible, a wedding present from his own father. He also prayed out loud for them, and his prayers were long. Dark storm clouds might fill the sky, while tons of hay lay waiting in the fields — precious food for the livestock that most farmers hurried to protect — but Mary's father never skipped or shortened his devotions. During these prayers, women and children had to keep silent.

Once, when all the Baker family had been down on their knees a long time, Mary opened her eyes

*Mark Baker's
entry in Bow
Union Church
records, 1822*

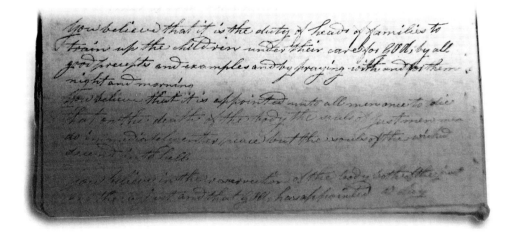

MARK BAKER

and saw, nearby, the pincushion full of long pins her mother used to keep her shawls in place. Quietly she reached out for one of them and then inched her way behind her father. One quick poke in the rear and she accomplished what nothing else could: the praying stopped!

Mark truly loved his six children and acted for their good, but he ruled them with an iron hand. When he decided what was right, he did not budge. Mark thought that God must be believed, feared, and obeyed. Unbelievers would suffer endless punishment, with no mercy or forgiveness. Most people were destined to go to a place called hell and there be damned forever. Mark urgently wanted his children to accept these teachings; otherwise, he feared, they would go to hell.

Mary listened silently to her father for years, but many questions troubled her. One time she dared to confront him directly. How can God punish people who do not know anything about Him, or those who do not believe in these teachings? None of her brothers and sisters had publicly accepted this faith. She did not want to be saved if they were condemned, driven away from God forever.

Mark argued long and hard. To his twelve-year-old daughter, his loud, unyielding voice fell like a curse on her brothers and sisters, and she became very ill. The family doctor, called to the house, said Mary had a high fever.

Her mom, bathing Mary's burning forehead, told her to lean on God's love. He would give her rest if she prayed to Him for an answer. Mary stopped listening to the argument raging inside her and turned with all her heart. As she prayed, a light, joyful feeling flooded over her, as though a big fire had been doused by cool water. The fever was gone. She got up and dressed, calm and well. Her mother was glad, the doctor quite amazed. Mary was no longer afraid of that horrible teaching, and never again did it have any power over her.

Mary's mother, Abigail Ambrose Baker, was good at smoothing things out. She listened to her husband's teaching about damnation, but that did not ruffle her own peaceful spirit. "Her presence, like the gentle dew and cheerful light, was felt by all around her," wrote a family friend.

Small and energetic, she went about managing her household, which included nine people to cook for, as well as many visitors who spent the night. Some of the family's clothes were made with wool from the Bakers' sheep. When the evenings turned cool, Abigail began the work of spinning. Mary felt at peace in her trundle bed, listening to the whirr of the wheel and her mother's 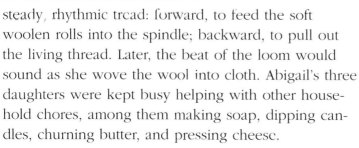 steady, rhythmic tread: forward, to feed the soft woolen rolls into the spindle; backward, to pull out the living thread. Later, the beat of the loom would sound as she wove the wool into cloth. Abigail's three daughters were kept busy helping with other household chores, among them making soap, dipping candles, churning butter, and pressing cheese.

Hardworking though she was, Abigail was keen to teach her children. Two of her favorite sayings were: "Count that day lost whose setting sun finds no good done," and, "It is more blessed to give than to receive."

Mary took these lessons to heart. One freezing winter day, she came home without her mittens or her cap. Her mother wondered where they were but said nothing. A few days later, the young girl ran shivering into the house. Now her coat was missing.

Mrs. Baker took the girl's cold face in her hands. "Mary, you know why you can't give all your warm clothes away, don't you? Mother does not have time to make others."

Mrs. Baker wanted her children to be honest. The walk home from school was through neighbor Gault's woods. One day Mary picked up a pitch pine knot, something the children loved to find because it blazed blue when thrown on the fire. It also kept the flame burning longer, which adults valued. Had Mary asked Mr. Gault for it, her mother questioned.

"No."

"Carry it right back again, Mary. It is stealing for you to do that, and God forbids you to steal."

"Must I carry it back now? I am so tired."

"Would you have God and Mother thinking until tomorrow that you had broken His commandment?"

When Mary was ten, the Bakers' oldest son, Samuel, married Eliza Ann Glover from Concord. Her brother, Major George Washington Glover, came to the wedding. He had such a long name his friends called him "Wash." To Mary he looked very much like her brother George, with his sandy red hair and easy manner. She stayed listening to the two friends as they joked together. Then, before she knew how it happened, Major Glover turned around and swept her up on his knee.

"How old are you?" he asked.

"Ten," Mary told him.

"Then I shall be back in five years," he laughed, "and wait for *you* to be my *wife.*"

Feeling embarrassed, Mary jumped off Wash's knee, but he quickly pulled out his gold pocket watch with its tiny gold key. It captivated her for a moment, as it lay shimmering in his hand, then she ran away and hid.

Four years later, Mark Baker decided it was time to sell the Bow farm and move closer to the town of Sanbornton Bridge, now called Tilton. Grandmother Baker had died the year before, and Mark's three sons had all left home, not wanting to be farmers. Living close to town would give his three girls better schooling and more social life.

Neither Abi nor Martha wanted to arrive at their new home in a wagon, so Mrs. Baker arranged rides for them with two young men who had carriages. Mary was left to trundle along with her parents in the old family wagon.

The Baker girls enjoyed meeting new people and received many invitations to dances and parties. They were not allowed to go to the dances, although Martha slipped out to a ball once, when their father was away. Abi especially liked her new life. "We see only the best people," she wrote to George.

Abi soon found a husband just suited to her — Alexander Tilton, the wealthiest mill owner in Sanbornton. When Abi and Alexander got married

the following year, who should come to the wedding but Wash Glover. Mary was fifteen by now.

"Bright, good and pure, aye brilliant!" her pastor and teacher, Rev. Enoch Corser, said of her. Mary was more used to young men by then, but Wash, who was always a jump ahead, surprised her again when he asked, would she write to him if he wrote to her, so they could get to know each other better? Letters were the only way to communicate over a long distance. Mary stayed outwardly calm, but she could not help smiling at the persistence of this handsome young man. She may have said yes, but letters between the two of them did not really start flowing until a few years later.

Wash was not the only one wanting letters. Her brother Albert, working hard away from home, wrote to his sisters, "If you knew how much satisfaction I take in reading your letters, you would write oftener...it is the *oasis* in the desert of life — the only spot upon which I rest with *entire* safety."

In 1836, Franklin Pierce was elected to the United States Senate from New Hampshire. The following year he was very glad to turn over his law office and the care of his parents to Albert, while he went off to Washington. In December 1838 he wrote to Albert, "I am anxious to hear again from my dear father. Do write two or three times a week in relation to the state of his health." Later, Franklin Pierce became the fourteenth President of the United States.

Albert himself entered politics in 1839 and served two years in the New Hampshire legislature. Having been raised on a farm, he was quick to stand by old neighbors like the Gaults, whose land was being cut up for the new railroads without proper payment.

It was not long before Albert became known for fairness, justice, and support of individual rights, and he received many invitations to speak in public. His workload in the office also increased.

"I have some eight or ten jury trials, double what I ever had before," he told his two younger sisters, and then added: "Your health is of paramount importance...I beg of you be careful." But it was Albert who became seriously ill. George went to be with him, but Albert died suddenly in 1841, when he was only thirty-one years old.

The Bakers were proud of Albert, but until his death even they did not realize how much he was liked and admired by his peers. As George sadly went over his brother's belongings, he found many letters from Albert's fellow politicians. George wrote to these men, asking them to return Albert's letters. Many heartfelt responses came in reply.

"Your brother," wrote one legislator, "was emphatically one of the best friends of the rights of the people."

"Not only was there a coincidence of political views between us, but we were personal friends," another commented.

The Baker family was in shock, and for Mary it was an empty, desolate time. All her life Albert had watched over her, guided and encouraged her. Now, he was gone.

CHAPTER THREE

Mountains and Valleys

Wash was working with Samuel, Mary's oldest brother, in his contracting business in Boston, when news came of a fire in Charleston, South Carolina, that had devastated several blocks in the center of the city. Generous loans were being offered by city officials to encourage rebuilding, and Wash decided to go there and try his luck. Always quick to make decisions, he sailed on the *Mohawk*, one of the first square-riggers to leave Boston after the fire.

Three weeks later, an advertisement in the Charleston *Mercury* announced that he and a partner were ready to "contract and build to the satisfaction of all who may favour them." A few weeks later, Wash announced that the partnership was dissolved, and he had "full authority."

Wash's advertisement in the Charleston Mercury.

In the summer of 1841, while she was on an errand in Sanbornton, Mary caught sight of her brother George looking particularly smart. She went up and slapped him on the back, saying, "Oh, you *are* dressed up!" When he turned around, it was George all right, but George Wash Glover! He had surprised her again. Mary went pink, but Wash seemed to enjoy her embarrassment. From that time on, his letters came more frequently.

Mr. Baker grumbled about this correspondence. He did not dislike Major Glover, but the prospect of his youngest child marrying and moving south was a grim one. Reports of fever epidemics in the hot, humid summer months convinced him that the climate was unhealthy, and he did not want her living so far away from home.

Early in 1843, Wash's letters stopped coming. Mary did not know what to make of it. Had she written something to offend him? Had his feelings toward her changed? She never suspected her father of intercepting the mail and burning the letters. She might have lost all contact with Wash, had her brother George not stepped in to help her.

George liked Wash Glover. He was convinced that

his friend was still writing to Mary. He explained his suspicions to his sad sister and proposed a plan. He was going on a business trip to the White Mountains in New Hampshire. Would Mary like to come? He would let Wash know, in advance, where they were going and where they would be staying.

At the first stop, Mary wrote in her journal of "the lonely night-wind," and "rain pelting the windows." The scenery was beautiful but "not the home for me." The next night was equally dreary. Then suddenly the young woman was in "much better health and spirits." She must have heard from Wash — a letter or two must have finally come through! As she jounced along in the coach the following day, Mary felt "at least midway between heaven and earth," and "such a sky-rocket adventure I never had."

Mary, quick-witted and lively, was slim, with curly brown hair and deep-set eyes. She had no lack of admirers among the young men at home, but somehow she was more intrigued by the tall, handsome Wash Glover.

Wash was a cheerful man who went about his work in a confident way. He wrote to George, "I believe among seven builders I am doing one-half of the Business in the City, last Saturday Bills to my workmen was $1267.00." Working in both Charleston and Wilmington, he and a new partner also had plans to build a cathedral in Haiti. But first Wash wanted to marry the youngest and loveliest Baker daughter, for whom he had waited twelve long years.

Slowly Mary's parents realized that she was going to marry Wash. They would have to let her go. Even the pull of her dear home circle could not hold her back now. Years later she said simply, "I married young the one I loved."

Mary and Wash were married on Sunday, December 10, 1843. The day was "some cloudy" as a local diary recorded, and this was Mary's mood, too — sadness mixed with excitement. The young couple waved good-bye to family and friends, the horse tossed his head, the harness jingled, and their sleigh glided swiftly away over the snowy New Hampshire roads.

Mary was as eager to take up her new life in the South, as Wash's friends were to welcome her. Wash had joined the Freemasons, an old, established, secret brotherhood. Following Bible teachings, Freemasons supported good works and upright business practices. Wash was well known and well liked by this network of friends, and his pretty northern bride was immediately admired and accepted.

Mary's strong interest in politics soon became known, and she was asked to write the toasts for one of the Democratic dinners, by the candidate for governor, Michael Hoke. She also wrote for the local newspapers, sending in her poems and enthusiastic articles about the South, and even a review of a local theater production. When her thoughts turned to home, she submitted her poem, "Old Man of the Mountain," which she had written on her trip with George the year before, to a new magazine for women writers called *The Floral Wreath*.

"Dear Child:" her mother wrote her, "We miss your good cheer. I look out at the window and say how I wish I could see

Old Man of the Mountain, Franconia, N.H., circa 1880

Above: Earliest known photograph of Mary, circa 1850

Right: George Washington Glover, "Wash" (ivory miniature portrait)

George and Mary coming over the hill... Mary, everything reminds me of you... Are you happy as you anticipated?"

Yes, in many ways, Mary could reply. But there was something that troubled her greatly in her new home — that black people were slaves to white people. Years earlier, Mary had marked in one of her reading books this poem by Cowper:

"I would not have a slave to till my ground,
To carry me, to fan me while I sleep,
And tremble when I wake, for all the wealth
That sinews bought and sold have ever earned."

Yet Wash used slaves, and the house he had built on Hasell Street and brought Mary to was a "single house," gracious and spacious in the front with slave quarters in the rear, designed to discourage runaways. Every newspaper Mary read had notices of runaway slaves, as well as advertisements that shocked her, such as "Negros and Furniture for Sale." A slave auction was held regularly at the Exchange, which was also the post office and located not far from the Glover home. It was illegal to free slaves in South Carolina, although some good friends of the Glovers, Rev. Gilman and his wife, bought young slaves on purpose to educate them and set them free.

Wash and Mary had been in Wilmington, North Carolina for several months, when suddenly in June, Wash faced disaster. He had put nearly all his money into building supplies for the proposed cathedral in Haiti. While these materials lay unprotected on the dock in Wilmington, news came that everything had

been lost — it was either burned or stolen.

Wash fell ill with yellow fever. Mary sat by him, day after day. She prayed desperately for her husband to get better, but after twelve days, he died. With his parting breath, he begged his brother Masons to "transport my beloved wife to her relatives." Mary was pregnant, and he wanted her safely back home with her family. She had been married less than a year.

After the funeral, the young widow stayed shut up in her room, eating very little and refusing to see anyone. A kindly Freemason, who insisted on seeing her, found her tear-stained and distraught. "What would your husband say to you if he came now and looked at you," he asked her. "What would he say to you for this action, and yielding to your agony of grief?" His words roused Mary and she got up saying it was all right — he could go away, he had done his work. She spent the next few weeks settling her husband's affairs, freeing his slaves. Later she explained, "I declined to sell them at his decease...for I could never believe that a human being was my property."

Wash's good friends did everything they could to help her, even to buying her clothes. True to their word, one of the Masons traveled with Mary as far north as New York. There to meet her was her brother, George. Even though New Hampshire was still several hundred miles to the north, just seeing him brought her the comfort of home. The steamy, inland journey with many changes from train to steamboat and again to train, had made the young widow weak and ill.

Mary's family opened their arms wide and took her back in. When her baby, Georgy, was born in September, she was still too weak to care for him. Mr. Baker sat for long hours by her bed. The family feared she might not live.

Georgy, on the other hand, grew sturdy and full of energy, like his father. Mahala Sanborn, a longtime friend and helper in the Baker home, had looked after Mary many times when she had been ill, and was fond of this loud little baby. To the family she seemed just the right person for Georgy, and he spent a great deal of time at her house.

Meanwhile, Mary had no money. What could she do to support herself and her little son? As the months went by and she grew stronger, the young Mrs. Glover decided to try a new venture.

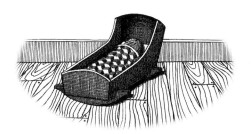

CHAPTER FOUR

Two Goodbyes

I go to Mrs. Glover
And tell her that I love her —

Mary Glover could not help smiling as the children
marched around the room singing this song. She had
opened a school. Encouraged by a minister friend,
Rev. Rust, she had started a kindergarten, one of the
first of its kind in New England. Abi and her husband
had a small building on their property in Sanbornton,
which had once been a shoemaker's shop. They had
it painted red, and fitted it with little chairs and desks.
Forty children flocked to this one room, with its plas-
ter walls and central brick chimney.

Sarah Clement, who lived in the house opposite, remembered running over to see her teacher as often as she could. Mary liked to work in her flower garden in the evenings, and the little girl would climb the gate and talk to her. To Sarah, Mrs. Glover, "tall, slender, exceedingly graceful, was altogether one of the most beautiful women I have ever seen." Sarah's mother and Mary were friends. "I often used to hear her talking to my mother and laughing. Her laugh was very sweet."

Mary was equally fond of Sarah, but one day when the girl was really naughty in school, she had to lay down the law. Sarah later wrote it was the one time she felt afraid of what her teacher would do. "Mrs. Glover said she would have to whip me so to go out and choose a stick. I went out in fear and trembling and brought in a little twig, the smallest I could find."

The contrite look on Sarah's face, and the ridiculous twig she brought in, made Mary want to laugh. She had no intention of whipping Sarah, but to make the lesson stick, she kept the laugh in and just told the girl to take her seat.

Although the children liked her school, Mary could not keep it going for long. She was not strong enough, and the school did not provide her with enough money. There was also Georgy to look after. At one time Abi was not well either and needed help caring for her son, Albert. Mary and her mother watched over the two boys as they romped and played in the Baker home.

"I feel as if I must *begin* something this summer, if my health is sufficient," Mary told Martha, still longing to be independent. But with no prospects, she turned again to writing, this time stories and more poems. Many of these were published, but that still did not bring in enough money to support herself and her son.

Mary and Georgy were living with the Bakers when Abi encouraged her parents to buy a lot in town and build a fine house near her. Mrs. Baker was not well and did not look forward to the upheaval of moving.

Early in November 1849, brother George came home and married his long-time girlfriend, Mathy Rand. A few weeks later, Mary had to write and tell him their mother had died. "This morning looks on us bereft of a Mother! Yes, that angel on earth is now in Heaven!... Oh! George, what is left of earth to *me!* But oh, my Mother! She has *suffered long with me;* let me be willing she should *rejoice,* and I bear on till I follow her."

After more than forty years of marriage, Mark Baker felt lonely and sad. As winter came along, he, Mary, and Georgy moved into the new house, but it seemed cold and damp without the cheery presence of his wife. His young grandson was too noisy to have around all the time. Mr. Baker even threatened to send him to the poorhouse, if Mary did not send him away herself.

Mary had nowhere to go. The following year, when her father decided to remarry, she knew both she and the boy had to leave. Abi offered to have Mary come and live in her house, but not Georgy — he was too rough-and-tumble. Redheaded Georgy was tall for his age, and he liked the outdoors. Her own son, Albert, was slight and delicate. She worried that his bigger cousin would overpower him.

North Groton, N.H.
where Georgy went
to live with Mahala
and Russell Cheney

What should be done with the boy, now a sturdy
six-year-old? Again the family thought of Mahala, who
had married Russell Cheney and was living about forty
miles away in North Groton. Mahala had no children
of her own and had always loved Mary's son. She
was delighted to have Georgy come and live with
them. Both Abi and Mr. Baker thought this an excel-
lent solution, but Mary dreaded the separation. What
else could she do, she wondered.

She sent the boy on a short visit to his Uncle and

Aunt Glover in nearby Concord, and wrote to them of the plan to send Georgy away to the Cheneys.

"Oh! How I *miss* him already! There seems nothing left me now to enjoy." And then she wrote, "I want very much to know how you have succeeded with him and if he has been a good boy (some naughty things of course)…but is he not a pretty good and very dear boy?… Will dear little Sully [the Glovers' son] be sorry to have him leave?"

Was she dropping a hint to her in-laws, hoping they would ask Georgy to live with them instead? They did not make the offer. Nothing, it seemed, would prevent the boy's move to North Groton.

The night before Georgy was to leave, Mary knelt by his side all the dark hours, hoping for some relief, but in the morning she knew he had to go. She packed his small belongings. As she waved goodbye to her son, Mary felt a stone in her heart, but she saw no other way.

CHAPTER FIVE

Another Marriage

Mary lived with her sister Abi for two years. Losing Georgy made her feel worse, not better, as Abi and her father had hoped. Often ill and in bed, she had plenty of time to think about her son. How she missed him and wanted him back!

When her father remarried, his new wife's relative, Daniel Patterson, came to live in Franklin, a town three miles away. Dr. Patterson, a dentist, was a handsome, outgoing man, who liked to wear fine clothes and impress the ladies. He rode his horse from town to town, doing whatever dental work was needed by the people there.

Mary was one of his patients. As their friendship grew, she wrote him little notes and even made up a funny poem about a toothache. Daniel at first tried writing fancy letters back, but he knew he could not keep it up for long. He was a plainspoken man. Better that Mary should know him as he really was, especially as he was beginning to hope she would marry him.

To Mary, the thought of marriage opened up a new world — to have, again, a devoted husband, a home of her own, and especially a place for Georgy. Mark Baker did not consider Daniel to be the right man for his daughter. In his view Daniel went to the wrong church — Baptist, not Congregational — and then there were rumors, "dark things," about his character.

Mary tossed and turned all night after her father voiced his doubts. She felt she could not change her religion, and the objections to Daniel's morals were troubling. She decided to break off the relationship.

"I beg you to remember that we will be *friends... Farewell*, May God bless you and protect you," she wrote. Daniel wanted to prove that he was worthy of her, but in the end just replied, "It seems that I have lost you at last..."

DANIEL PATTERSON

But all was not lost as he thought. As a dentist, he still worked on Mrs. Glover's teeth, and that gave him the chance to work on her heart. She so wanted a home for Georgy. When Daniel promised him a home, if only she would marry him, Mary's doubts were swept away.

On her wedding day, before the ceremony, Mary signed a paper naming her future husband as Georgy's guardian. Daniel and Mark Baker both signed a guardianship bond the same day. To make the bond legal, Daniel had to appear in court. He never went. He wanted to please his wife, but he did not always carry through on his promises.

More than two years passed. Finally, Mary persuaded Daniel to move to North Groton, where

Georgy still lived with the Cheneys. Her sister Martha dipped into her meager resources and loaned them money for a house.

North Groton, in the foothills of the White Mountains, was a farming community of about a thousand people. It had a square, white church and a one-room, overcrowded school. Mary and Daniel found a small cottage built on a high rock and granite foundation, the site of a previous mill. A rushing stream flowed swiftly right under the kitchen window. Here Mary looked forward to reuniting with her tall, active, eleven-year-old son. He, in turn, wanted to be with his mother. Mahala had taken him from time to time to visit Mary in the past, and he remembered sitting on her knee, listening to Bible stories. Now here she was, living only a mile away.

Mary hoped to teach him to read stories on his own, but he balked at the lessons. Georgy disliked the noisy village school and did not fit in with the other children. He was an outsider. He preferred hanging around the blacksmith's shop, or going fishing, or skipping stones on the pond. When he looked at the stones carefully, he noticed their pretty colors. North Groton had many gemstones — amethysts, aquamarines, garnets, rose quartz, and crystals. Georgy started a collection, which he kept

Patterson house, North Groton, N.H.

PHOTO BY GORDON CONVERSE

North Groton center, showing schoolhouse with flag, circa 1900

hidden in the barn at the Cheney farm. Russell Cheney, Mahala's husband, made him work on the farm, another reason he had not learned to read.

Daniel and Mary argued about the boy. Daniel felt his wife's efforts were wasted on Georgy, and that his visits only left her tired and weak. She, in turn, grieved and worried that her son was not getting the education he needed. She had left her family and circle of friends to be with Georgy. She must see him and teach him. In spite of all her pleas, Daniel insisted it was best for her that the boy stay away.

One day Mahala and Georgy slipped in to see Mary while Daniel was gone from home. As they were leaving, Daniel unexpectedly returned and was furious to see his stepson in the yard. He went after the boy with his stout stick. Georgy ran around the house, picked up a stone, and threw it hard. It glanced off Daniel's shoulder, shattering a window. The break that followed was much harder to fix than a windowpane.

Abi had her hands full at home, but she made the forty-mile trip north in her carriage to see what was going on with Georgy. Mary was glad for her visit and did not suspect its purpose. Unknown to her, Abi and Daniel may have spoken to Mahala and Russell about the Cheneys' hopes to go out west to Minnesota. Russell's brother and several other New Hampshire families were already successfully farming there. Lack of money had prevented the Cheneys from going in the past. Now, after Abi's visit, they found the means to go, and Georgy would go with them.

—ɯ—

The first that Mary heard of this was when the boy came to give her a quick kiss goodbye and started to cry. He did not want to leave his mother, and Cheney had made him throw away his whole rock collection. Mary was overcome by news of another separation. They were being forced apart again. It felt like a family plot.

The Cheneys went back to Sanbornton Bridge to say goodbye to relatives and friends, then took the long, six-day journey by train to the Mississippi River, and from there the riverboat to Winona, Minnesota. Georgy, still rebellious and unhappy about leaving his mother, insisted he was going to try and find her. To keep him quiet, Mary learned later, Russell Cheney told him it was no use — she was dead.

After Georgy left, a storm of sorrow engulfed
his mother. She could barely sit up. All contact with
Georgy was cut. Try as she might, she could not
locate him. On top of this, Daniel told her he had to
travel again to find work to support them. Mary was
left in the care of Myra Smith, a young, blind woman
who was devoted to her.

Every pleasant day Myra carefully wrapped blankets
around Mary. Then she pulled her out in her rocker
onto the piazza, a small wooden porch on the side
of the house. Here Mary would stay as long as she
could. From the piazza she became friendly with Daniel
Kidder, her closest neighbor. Kidder was 18 when Mary
and her husband moved in. He was impressed by this
"fine looking woman, intellectual and stately in appear-
ance...[who] kept her house in the most perfect order."
He was intrigued that she wrote poetry for the maga-
zines of the day. Mary, unable to help her own son
to read, "took a great interest in the education of the
young then living near her," Kidder wrote. "She was a
great help to me in my studies at that time. I remember
her as a sincere friend."

Myra's sister, Marcia, who was ten in 1859, was
also a frequent visitor. She wrote that Mrs. Patterson
was ill nearly all the time, lying in bed, with a book
for her constant companion. Mrs. Patterson would
"call me to her room, lay down her book, and place
her thin white hand on my head or stroke my cheek.
She wished to comfort me, for I had lately lost a good
father."

Once Mary could not help exclaiming, "Oh, you
dear little girl. You are worth your weight in gold. I
wish you were mine!"

The children in the neighborhood, fascinated by the
"poor sick lady," as they called Mary, loved to bring in

the earliest berries and flowers for her. But the adults were less openhearted. In that farming community, people were concerned with how much a cow would fetch, when to dig the potatoes, and the price of a cord of wood. It was hard for them to understand what a woman did who lay in bed all day.

Actually Mary was busy. She read her Bible almost constantly. Still seeking a cure for herself and others, she also delved into homeopathy, a popular system in those days. Daniel, her husband, was a homeopathist, so she was familiar with some of the ideas. In homeopathy, the art of curing was founded on resemblances, "like cures like." It was believed that a drug that created symptoms similar to those of a sick patient could be used to cure that patient. The more diluted the drug, the more powerful it was thought to be. Mary's medical experiments led her to make her own pills.

A neighbor who was ill with dropsy took some pills that Mary prescribed and started to feel better. Mary feared the drug was too strong and wanted to stop the pills. The woman tried going without them but got worse. Mary later wrote: "It then occurred to me to give her unmedicated pellets and watch the results… She went on in this way, taking the unmedicated pellets — and receiving occasional visits from me — but employing no other means, and she was cured."

From the way this woman responded, Mary began to see that it was not the drug, but the woman's faith in the medicine that brought about a cure. Still Mary was unable to help herself.

Eventually Dr. Patterson had to stay home and nurse his "very dear wife." With no work, and no income, the Pattersons could no longer repay Mary's sister Martha the money they owed on the house. The doctor often had money problems with the local farmers, too.

One time Daniel bargained for a load of wood from his neighbor, Joseph Wheet. Weeks passed and he still had not paid for it. One day, as Daniel was in the dooryard splitting the wood, Wheet and his son, Charles, happened to drive by. Joseph stopped his wagon, walked over to the doctor, and asked for his money. Mary heard angry voices, then the sound of blows. Horrified, she watched the two men roll over and over while Charles stood by, axe in hand, ready to strike at Daniel. Unconscious of everything but the need to save her husband, she sprang up, ran out,

and seized the axe from the boy. Under the headline "FEMALE BRAVERY," the *Nashua Gazette* published a dramatic account of the story in its March 15 issue, ending with: "Help soon came, the assailants fled, and the feeble but brave wife was carried back to bed."

When the Pattersons finally left North Groton, it was a terrible, humiliating day for Mary. She was forced to sell some of her furniture to cover their debts. Worse still, even though the Wheets were made to stand trial, they took possession of the house and tolled the church bell in triumph as Mary left the village. Daniel was away. Abi and Martha both came to their sister's rescue, fetching her in Abi's carriage.

"It was spring and the roads were very bad — in spots deep snow — other places mud," remembered Myra, Mary's blind housekeeper. This faithful woman trudged behind the carriage down the steep mountain road, six long miles to Rumney, their destination. Abi walked partway with her, both of them unable to bear Mary's "moans and grief."

CHAPTER SIX

Prison Breaks

The carriage with Mary, Martha, and Abi inside, Myra still following on foot, stopped in front of the Herberts' boarding-house, where Daniel had rented rooms. There her sisters had to leave her. Soon Daniel came back, started up his dental practice again, and somehow managed to find them a house of their own, away from the gossip and curiosity of the other boarders.

The new house lifted Mary's spirits. Rumney was no bigger than North Groton, but because it had a train station, there were more connections to the outside world. Rumblings of the Civil War and the growing divide between North and South reached Mary through the newspapers. She read of the secession of South Carolina, the upheavals in Charleston (her first southern city), and Major Anderson's secret withdrawal to Fort Sumter in the middle of the harbor. She heard how the Major had withheld firing on the Southerners, hoping to prevent a war, but in the end had been forced to fire back for self-protection. Then followed Fort Sumter's capture — for the South a first victory, for the North a sad surrender.

Stirred by this news Mary wrote a long poem, "Major Anderson and Our Country," which was published in *The Independent Democrat* of Concord, February 14, 1861. One verse read:

> Yet would I yield a husband, child, to fight,
> Or die the unyielding guardians of right,
> Than that the life blood circling through their
>   veins,
> Should warm a heart to forge new human chains.

Little did she know that both her husband and child would soon be involved in the war, and because of this, she would finally have news of Georgy.

When Fort Sumter fell to the Confederates in 1861, the governor of Minnesota happened to be in Washington. He immediately went to see President Lincoln and was the first state governor to offer assistance. Back in Minnesota rallies were held, flags were sold out, and many young men enlisted for the army. Georgy Glover, two days under the age of seventeen, was one of them. The Minnesota quota of men filled so quickly, Georgy had to cross into Wisconsin where he joined the Eighth

Georgy Glover, shortly after enlisting in the Eighth Wisconsin Infantry

Wisconsin Infantry, called the Eagle Regiment.

Right after enlisting, Georgy and other new recruits walked 179 miles to Camp Randall in Madison, Wisconsin. In his inside coat pocket, the new infantryman put his Bible, with a picture of his mother carefully kept in the front. And although he lost some of his equipment along the way, he carried his pocket Bible and a Sunday school hymnal all the time he was in service.

Perhaps because Georgy was going to war,

Cheney let him know that his mother had not died. When Georgy joined his regiment, a young man named David Hall enlisted at the same time. David wrote letters home for soldiers who could not write themselves. He may have written Georgy's first letter home to Mary. How delighted she was to receive news of him! Although Georgy and his mother did not see each other for another eighteen years, they could now keep in contact through letters.

Mary's husband got into the war in a totally different way. Money had been collected in New Hampshire for Southerners who supported the North. The state governor commissioned Daniel to take the funds down to Washington. When he arrived, he went to see the battlefield at Bull Run, got too close to the fighting, and was captured.

"You will be amazed to learn that I am in prison," he wrote to his wife. His letter ended with, "My anxiety for you is intense but be of as good cheer as possible and trust in God." Mary's concern for her husband was equally great. She wrote letters to everyone she could think of, including ex-President Franklin Pierce, hoping to get Daniel released through an exchange of prisoners, but with no success.

Meanwhile, Mary was still working on her own release from illness. Before Daniel left for the South, he had heard of a man named Phineas Quimby in Portland, Maine. Quimby, a clockmaker, had become interested in hypnotism as a means to help people, and his fame for remarkable cures was widespread. Daniel had written to Quimby, hoping to arrange a meeting between him and Mary, but nothing came of it. Now Mary decided to go to Portland and see him for herself.

The invalid had to stop and rest many times, as she slowly got dressed for the journey. Samuel, her oldest brother, and his wife came from Boston to take her to Portland. Mary had to be carried up to her room when they arrived at the International Hotel, where Quimby lived and worked. Yet her hopes were high. She had come here to regain a sense of life.

PHINEAS QUIMBY

There were others in the waiting room when Mary went in, but her thoughts were fixed solely on the small, energetic doctor. Quimby was a kindly man who had a piercing look. He was called a magnetic healer, because he believed that energy — in the form of electricity — passed from himself to his patient. In his opinion, dipping his hands in water and rubbing parts of the patient's body aided this effect.

Charles Norton, a medical student, whose mother was a patient of Quimby when he worked in Bangor,

Maine, made notes on how the doctor worked. He walked among his patients and "in a loud voice demanded that each patient look him straight in the eye. An assistant followed him about the room holding a large dish of water. In most cases not a question was asked, in some, however, Mr. Quimby would say, 'Where is your pain... What ails you?' In some [cases], he would wet both hands in the water and gently press or stroke the face, neck or head of the person being treated. In a number of incidences he would say, in a quick, sharp voice: 'Get up and walk away! You can walk, walk!' the patient almost always doing as bid."

The doctor practiced a form of hypnotism or mesmerism, controlling his patients' thoughts.

Mary watched intently, feeling better already. When it came to her turn, Quimby told her that she was held in bondage by the opinions of her family and physicians. He dipped his hands in water and vigorously rubbed her head.

"I well remember the fearful tangle which Mrs. Patterson's hair was in after her treatments, "her landlady, Martha Hunter, wrote later," and often helped her to comb it out." Undergoing this treatment, Mary was free from the pain in her spine for the first time in years. In a week she was able to climb the 182 steps leading to the dome of Portland City Hall. After bouts of being bedridden for so many years, this must have felt like flying.

Mary wrote enthusiastically about Quimby in the Portland *Evening Courier*. She tried to find out how he healed people, and made many notes. Were his healings the same as those of Jesus in the Bible? Unlike Jesus, Quimby based his cures not on God but on himself. Many of his patients, including Mary, found

*Portland City
Hall, 1864*

that while they were with Quimby, they felt better. When they left him, old ills returned. His patients needed constant reinforcement from the doctor.

Quimby's methods confirmed for Mary what she had been thinking about for a long time. She remembered the woman she had healed with unmedicated pellets in North Groton, and her own sudden strength when the Wheets had threatened Daniel. As she later wrote, "During twenty years,...I had been trying to trace all physical effects to a mental cause."

Mary was about to go to Washington to press for Daniel's release, when she heard that he had escaped from prison and was coming back North. Daniel joined Mary in Portland and decided to start up his dental practice in Lynn, Massachusetts. He also wanted to go around giving talks on "what he heard and saw among the rebels."

Georgy was severely wounded at the battle of Corinth, Mississippi, in October 1862. His regiment

47

had made a rapid march and fought four hours the first day. At dawn the following morning, their line was under heavy fire, and they lost many men. Georgy helped man a cannon and was wounded in the neck. He was hospitalized many weeks. Mary wrote him comforting letters and was overjoyed when he recovered.

In 1865 Mary lost her father, Mark Baker. His will, following the custom of those days, left the bulk of his money and property to his son George. Although his two younger daughters, Martha and Mary, were desperately poor, Mark felt it was enough to have supported them during his lifetime. Each of his three girls received only $1.00, and two of them were given a piece of furniture.

A few months later Quimby, who had been ill for some time, also died. Mary felt abandoned. All her supports were going, one by one. Yet, she was about to face an experience that changed the course of her life.

1862 dollar bill depicting Salmon Chase, who caused the motto "In God We Trust" to be put on U.S. coinage.

CHAPTER SEVEN

A Turning Point

On a cold February night in 1866, when Mary was walking to a temperance meeting with her friends in Lynn, she slipped on some ice and fell, striking her back and head. As she was unconscious, her companions quickly carried her to the nearest house, owned by Samuel Bubier. Dr. Cushing, a popular homeopathist and surgeon, was called. He came twice that evening. Mary had a concussion and possible spinal dislocation, he said gravely. While she lay speechless and unmoving that night, some of her friends stayed and watched over her, along with Mrs. Bubier.

The next day Mary "came to consciousness," as she later wrote, "amid a storm of vapors from

The Bubier home where Mary was taken after she fell at the corner of Oxford and Market streets (bottom right)

cologne, chloroform, ether, camphor etc., but to find myself the helpless cripple I was before I saw Dr. Quimby." She insisted, however, on being taken home. Those who had kept watch were afraid for her, and the doctor was very reluctant to let her go. He gave her an eighth of a grain of morphine, and while she was plunged in sleep, they took her by sleigh to her own home.

Dr. Cushing stayed with her until she regained consciousness a second time. Still no improvement. The following day her minister, Rev. Clark, came to pray with her and prepare her for the worst. A close friend, Rebecca Brown, also visited Mary, bringing her nine-year-old daughter, Arietta. According to Arietta, as they were leaving, Mary astonished them by saying, "When you come down the next time, I will be sitting up in the next room. I am going to walk in."

"Mary, what on earth are you talking about!" Arietta remembered her mother exclaiming.

Lying helpless in bed that afternoon, Mary asked to be left alone. She opened her Bible at random and found herself reading the story of a man who could not walk. "The shadow of the dark valley gathered round me," so that she could hardly see the words on the page. Then she read how Jesus healed that man, telling him "Arise," and walk.

Jesus' saying, "I am the way, the truth, and the life," came with such a blaze of understanding, that she felt a power and strength that were not her own. When next she thought about her body, the coldness and piercing pain had ceased. She was able to get up and walk into the next room.

Her friends, waiting for her to die, were astonished. Rev. Clark returned, and when Mary met him at the door, he wondered, am I seeing a ghost? No. This was Mary herself,

> ### ST. MATTHEW
> *One sick of the palsy cured.*
>
> #### CHAPTER IX.
>
> AND he entered into a ship, and passed over, and came into his own city.
>
> 2 And, behold, they brought to him a man sick of the palsy, lying on a bed: and Jesus seeing their faith said unto the sick of the palsy; Son, be of good cheer; thy sins be forgiven thee.
>
> 3 And, behold, certain of the scribes said within themselves, This *man* blasphemeth.
>
> 4 And Jesus knowing their thoughts said, Wherefore think ye evil in your hearts?
>
> 5 For whether is easier, to say, *Thy* sins be forgiven thee; or to say, Arise, and walk?
>
> 6 But that ye may know that the Son of man hath power on earth to forgive sins, (then saith he to the sick of the palsy,) Arise, take up thy bed, and go unto thine house.
>
> 7 And he arose, and departed to his house.
>
> 8 But when the multitudes saw *it*, they marvelled, and glorified God, which had given such power unto men.

feeling she was made new. The next day Mary sent for Dr. Cushing to show him she was well.

1851 King James Bible (partial page)

"What! Are you about?" He was astounded. Was it his medicine that had healed her?

"Come here and I will show you." Mary took him to her dresser and opened the drawer. Every bit of medicine was left there, untouched.

"If you will tell me how you cured yourself, I will lay aside drugs and never prescribe another dose of medicine," he told her.

But Mary did not know herself how she had been healed, or if other people could be helped in this way. Was this the same presence she had known as a little girl, when the voice called her name and she had answered? She had felt the same lifting love, which had freed her so quickly from the fever. Only now the loving presence was much stronger.

CHAPTER EIGHT

"I Found Him"

Mary felt herself being led, like a little child, into a new world of light and life. Just as a small stream ripples over pebbles and rocks, so came her first thoughts. But still there were times when she looked back at past troubles and felt afraid. At one point she wrote urgently to Julius Dresser, one of Quimby's patients, who had taken an interest in healing: "I am constantly wishing that *you* would step forward into the place he [Quimby] has vacated. I believe you would do a vast amount of good. I confess I am frightened... Now can't *you* help me?"

But Dresser refused, saying, "I do not even help my wife out of her trouble."

With that path blocked, there was no turning back. Mary could no longer depend on another person. She had only one familiar guide from the past — her Bible. With new eyes she searched it every day for answers. What did the Bible teach about God and healing?

Meanwhile, her husband was no support. Daniel disappeared with one of his patients, the wife of a rich businessman in Lynn. The man, in anger, chased after them, brought his wife back, and kept her locked in a room. With the aid of her servants, the woman escaped one day and went to see Mary.

Mary already felt wronged and hurt by this woman. Why had she come to see her?

"I came because of what your husband has told me of you," the wife replied. "I knew you must be a good woman and I felt you would help me." She begged Mary to talk with the angry husband. Mary met with the man, and his heart softened. He forgave his wife and they went back to living together again.

But the Pattersons' marriage was over. Daniel had left her one time too often. There had been too much "disappointment and tears," Mary told her sister Martha. Daniel went back to Sanbornton Bridge. It was probably Abi who persuaded him to give Mary $200 a year in support. But Daniel's payments were as erratic as his life. They soon stopped.

Daniel drifted around in later life. He spoke of his wife as a pure, Christian woman. He blamed himself for their separation and later told a friend that "if he had done as he ought he might have had a pleasant and happy home as one could wish for."

For her part, Mary still cared about Daniel. She wrote to a friend to find out how he was doing and whether he had found a place to live. Now that he was gone for good, she felt very much on her own. In September 1866 she wrote a poem, "I'm Sitting Alone," that was later printed in the *Lynn Reporter*. In it she thinks of her mother, "parting the curls to kiss my cheek;" of her first husband, Wash; and herself as a "fair young bride." She writes of Georgy's "glad young face upturned to his mother's in playfulness." All that has gone. Yet even in some of her saddest poems, Mary ends on an upbeat. This time she concludes with:

And wishing this earth more gifts from above,
Our reason made right, and hearts all love.

Mary asks for right reasoning and a heart full of love. In spite of very little money and no settled place to live, she still had two thoughts uppermost: what had brought about her own healing, and how to relieve the sufferings of others.

Abi, who always looked for a way to help her younger sister, wrote to Mary. "We will build a house for you next to our own and settle an income upon you. We can be together very much and you can pursue your writing." But there was one condition — Mary must give up her strange ideas about divine healing.

Mary was lonely for her family and a circle of friends, but there was only one way she could reply: "I must do the work God has called me to." She could not bow to Abi's will. In the past Mary had always listened to her sister; now she had to turn her down. Abi's pride was hurt.

One summer day in 1866, Mary went for a walk on one of the beaches in Lynn. A woman had left her seven-year-old son, George, sitting on the sand, while she went to hitch up their horse and get some water. He had been carried on a pillow since birth, as both of his feet were turned backward, and he had never walked. When his mother came back, the boy had disappeared. Then, to her astonishment, she spotted him down by the water, with a stranger holding both his hands. As she watched, Mary let go, and George for the first time stood on his own. Then he took a few steps by himself. The mother ran over to them. The two women looked deep into each other's eyes, then, crying with happiness, they gave thanks to God.

Later, a family friend wrote down the boy's description of what happened. He told of a strange lady walking by, and "seeing him stretched upon the pillow with

his feet covered, asked why he was not playing with the other children there. He told her he had never walked, and she lifted the shawl and saw why. She put her hands under his arms, and while he protested his inability to do so, told him to stand, and when he was lifted to an upright position, she guided his feet with her own, supporting him the while he took his first feeble steps into freedom." The size and shape of George Norton's feet soon became completely normal. He grew up to become a mechanical engineer and led a happy life.

Experiences like this one convinced Mary she must be on the right track. She found that filling her thoughts with God's infinite power and love destroyed her fear of sickness and healed people. Was there a science to this method of healing? Could it be used by anybody? She knew from the Bible that many people had been healed through "holy, uplifting faith." But, she felt, "I must know the Science of this healing."

"I sought God diligently," she wrote, "and with the

Bible in my hand, searching its precious pages, I found Him…all nature declaring God is wisdom, God is Love."

Mary was eager to try out her ideas on anyone who would listen. They were so revolutionary, that even her most spiritually minded friends feared she would be thought insane if she persisted. So she turned to the new people she met.

At one time Mary boarded with a Mrs. Ellis and her schoolteacher son, Fred. He recounted how she would spend all day in her room writing, and in the evening, "would read the pages to Mother and me, inviting, almost demanding, our criticism and suggestions."

Thirty years later, Fred wrote to Mary of his "cherished remembrance of those precious evenings in the little sitting-room at Swampscott, when the words of Jesus, of Truth, were so illumined by your inspired interpretation."

And she wrote back, "Do you forget your Christmas present to me — that basket of kindlings all split by your hand and left at my door? I do not."

But few of the places Mary stayed were as warm and friendly as the Ellises. Most boarders in rooming houses worked at a job during the day. In the evening they sat around the supper table, relaxed, talking. Very few of them understood what Mary was doing. What was this lady all about, reading her Bible all day long, making notes, coming up with funny ideas about God and healing?

CHAPTER NINE

A Shoemaker Learns a New Trade

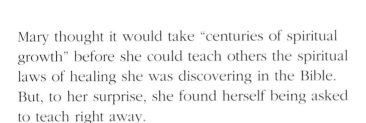

Mary thought it would take "centuries of spiritual growth" before she could teach others the spiritual laws of healing she was discovering in the Bible. But, to her surprise, she found herself being asked to teach right away.

Hiram Crafts, a young shoemaker, came with his wife, Mary, to work in the shoe factories in Lynn part of each year. In early winter they returned to their home in East Stoughton, Massachusetts, to join farmers and other men working in their backyard shoe shops. Hiram and his wife were both Spiritualists. They believed that the spirits of people who had died could control those who were living. They thought that a medium, that is someone sensitive and tuned in to the "spirit world," could receive communications from the dead about the past and the future and in this way guide and direct the living.

Mary met the Crafts while staying at the same boarding house in Lynn. When she talked about her ideas on spiritual healing at the supper table, she found Hiram a ready listener.

In November, Hiram begged Mary to come back to

East Stoughton with him and his wife, so he could learn to be a healer. Mary was a little reluctant to move in with the Crafts at first, but Hiram was so insistent that she agreed to go. She took what was left of her furniture to furnish their front parlor and began teaching Hiram in return for her room and board.

Hiram wrote later that he changed his views and gave up spiritualism as a result of Mary's teaching. "We had nothing but the New Testament, and had no manuscripts of any kind until after I had been studying six months," he explained. Mary started with the first book of the New Testament, Matthew, and made notes, verse-by-verse, of what she learned of its spiritual meaning, and taught this to Hiram.

Both teacher and student did well, and in a few months the Crafts and Mary moved to a more comfortable house in nearby Taunton. As this was a much larger town, Hiram expected more patients. He put an advertisement in the paper and addressed it, "To The Sick."

"I can cure you," he said, and then gave a list of diseases. "If you give me a fair trial and are not helped, I will refund your money." At the end of the advertisement was a statement from Abigail Raymond of Taunton, who had been cured of a longstanding illness by Hiram. Mary helped Hiram by taking the more difficult cases herself.

James Ingham, who felt he "was surely going down the victim of consumption," wrote, "I had not received her attention but a short time, when my bad symptoms disappeared, and I regained health. During this time, I rode out in storms to visit her, and found the damp weather had no effect on me. From my personal experience I am led to believe the science by which she not only heals the sick, but explains the way to keep well, is deserving of the earnest attention of community; her cures are not the result of medicine, mediumship, or mesmerism, but the application of a Principle that she understands."

James Ingham meant that Mary did not use drugs. She did not rely on a medium, someone directed by spirits of the dead, nor mesmerism, which is a form of hypnotism. She relied on God as the healing Principle.

Mary wrote to her sister Martha about her own and Hiram's success: "All that come to him sick he cures." Perhaps that is why when Ellen, Martha's twenty-one-year-old daughter, lay ill with enteritis, Martha sent for her sister. Ellen, given up by three doctors, was said to be dying. Bark and straw were spread on the road outside the house to prevent her from being jolted by carts rolling by. Anyone going into the young woman's room stepped on tiptoe. She could only be moved from bed to bed on a sheet. Most of the time she lay silently with her eyes closed.

ELLEN PILSBURY

Mary went into the room and turned her thoughts over completely to God's caring love. In a few minutes she heard Ellen say, "I am glad to see you, Aunty." Mary kept on praying and then told her niece to get up and walk, and then to stamp her foot strongly on the floor. Ellen walked across the room seven times, stamped her foot hard, and felt no ill effects. The next day she was dressed and went down to the table.

"Such a change came over the household," a family member wrote later. "We all felt 'the angel of the Lord appeared and glory shone round.'"

Abi was away at a fashionable resort, where the rich gathered to drink natural mineral water for their health, so she missed Mary's visit. The oldest sister had mixed feelings when she heard how Mary had healed their niece. She wrote to Martha a few days later, "I have my private opinion that in the end no real good will result from all the stir she has made about Ellen, but hope I am mistaken and great benefit will result from her efforts yet."

Abi was right. The family chose not to benefit from Ellen's experience, but great good for others, in the form of healing, did result from Mary's efforts.

Ellen joined her Aunt Mary when she returned to the Crafts' household in Taunton. When they arrived they found the couple in turmoil. Mrs. Crafts was tired of "doing" for her houseguest, and the niece was just an added burden. She wanted Hiram to go back to shoemaking, a more respectable, lasting trade.

Hiram was supposed to give Ellen continued treatments until her health was on a firm basis, but he did not know what to do with his angry wife. In this upset house Ellen was confused. The joy of her sudden recovery evaporated. She felt shame that her aunt lived with these poor, uneducated people. The only way to keep her dignity was to go home and forget the whole thing. She went, without a good word for her aunt, resentful that she even owed her gratitude for the healing.

Mary also left the Crafts. They returned to East Stoughton, where Hiram went back to shoemaking.

Shoemakers at work, engraving circa 1872

When Mary wrote to him a year later to see if he would like to resume working with her, he answered: "I should be willing to do all you ask if I was in different circumstances. I feel the same interest in the developing of Truth and its principles… But it would be impossible for me to come over there to help you at present. I should have no peace at home if I did."

In spite of this setback with Ellen and the Crafts, Mary knew she had to go on with the work. She saw the effect of her teaching: on one side, great gratitude for healing and a desire to learn more, from people like Hiram; on the other, anger and open hostility, from people like Ellen and Mrs. Crafts.

She also saw her own life on two levels. Her Bible search was "sweet, calm and buoyant with hope" — that was her inner life. Hard living conditions, no home, few friends, and barely scraping together enough money to live on — that was her outer life. Each time a sadness or disappointment tried to swamp her, she found herself lifted up by trusting God.

ALANSON WENTWORTH

SALLY WENTWORTH

After the Crafts, Mary moved to several new places. Then, in the fall of 1868, she received an enthusiastic invitation to stay with the Wentworths, whom she had met through Hiram in East Stoughton. Each member of that family found her fascinating for a different reason.

Alanson, the father, who was part-farmer, part-shoemaker, was devoted to his Bible. He loved to hear Mary's comments on Scripture. He was grateful when she healed him of sciatica in his hip, freeing him to work again. Sally, the mother, loved to tend the sick, and she looked forward to learning about healing from Mary. One of the three children, Lucy, then about thirteen, adored Mary, and wanted to be with her all the time.

Mary called her "little Lue," and let the young girl wear her pearl ring, which, to Lucy, was a great favor. Often Mary went to meet her on her way home from school, and they would walk across the fields to Aunt Lucy Porter's ancient house. The spacious old house, with its brook flowing by, was a welcome change for Mary after being shut up writing in her room all day. Aunt Porter made her feel relaxed and peaceful.

In the evenings Lucy and Mary read together or played games. Mary bought the Wentworths a backgammon board and taught them how to play. Charles, Lucy's seventeen-year-old brother, and his friends, would often join in the fun, and then times would be more boisterous. William Scott, Charles' friend wrote:

"Two or three nights out of every week...I used to visit Mrs. [Glover] with other young folks of the town...to listen to her talks, for even then she was regarded by those who knew her as a wonderful woman." Charles called Mary "cheerful, sprightly," and said her stay with his family was "one of the brightest spots in my life."

Mary enjoyed young people's company. "She was lively and entered heartily into our fun and made herself one of us," Lucy said. But she also remembered times when Mary was discouraged by her life. With a face full of misery she would repeat a poem of Longfellow:

LUCY WENTWORTH

> The day is cold, and dark, and dreary;
> It rains, and the wind is never weary.
> The vine still clings to the mouldering wall,
> But at every gust the dead leaves fall,
> And the day is dark and dreary.

"Then," the young girl said, "it would take all my childish ingenuity and affection to bring her back to her old self again."

Lucy was intrigued by the way Mary walked, "a sort of graceful glide," and although her older friend had few fine clothes, "It made no difference what she wore, there always seemed to be a certain style about her."

Mary told Lucy about Wash, her dashing first husband of only six months, and Georgy, their son, whom she had lost when he had been moved to Minnesota. She let her know about Daniel, her second husband, how attractive he was to other women, and how he had left her.

Many years later Lucy wrote that Mary explained the ups and downs of her life in this way: "Beauty, Order and Harmony are the sweet rhythm of nature. They join hands with the green earth and glorious firmament in one continuous page of nature's bright and living characters." But then she went on, "Harmony has an opposite discord. And the false is the opposite of the true. When malice looks upon love, the scene changes, the vision fades, for the serpent has entered the garden of life, and driven away the beautiful hours of friendship and the sweet sunshine of the soul."

Mary sensed that some day, she and Lucy might not remain friends. Lucy explains: "The morning she was about to leave us, she took me in her arms and said, 'Well, little Lue, I feel as years go by, that *you* will turn against me, but try and remember what we have been to each other,' she kissed me and so passed out of my life forever." Lucy wrote about her long-ago friend more than fifty years later, but her heart still ached that they had never met again.

CHAPTER TEN

Writing Her Book

☞ MRS. GLOVER, the well-known SCIENTIST, will receive applications for one week from ladies and gentlemen who wish to learn how to HEAL THE SICK without medicine, and with a success unequaled by any known method of the present day, at DR. KENNEDY'S OFFICE, No 71 South Common street, Lynn, Mass.   aug10-3t*

This was the advertisement Mary placed in the *Lynn Semi-Weekly Reporter* on August 13, 1870.

She taught in the evening, because many of her students were in the shoe trade and had to work during the day. They came to her class with their hands stained and worn, but with their minds open for something new. Sitting around a plain wooden table, with only a single lamp casting long shadows, and with insects banging up against the windows, they found to their surprise that learning to heal meant learning about God.

"What is God?" was the first question. Many people imagined God as a man with a beard somewhere up

in the sky. Mary understood God to be "Principle, wisdom, love and truth." Being under the law of God leads naturally to healing and peace. Mary put down these ideas in a small book she called, *The Science of Man*. Each student received a handwritten copy, which he had to study thoroughly, and even memorize. Mary used a question and answer method, which let her see just what each one was thinking. Everyone participated. People felt their thoughts stirred up, their old beliefs challenged.

"While we may have been unable to fully grasp the truths," one student wrote, "we could not fail to realize the inspiration."

The course consisted of twelve lessons, but Mary freely gave additional classes and private teaching to her pupils. Each week, past students gathered for refresher meetings and advice from their teacher. She urged them to be honest, loving, and pure in order to have any understanding of God. They must seek the truth as a means of doing good. That would lead to better healing. If they were just looking to make money, their patients would not recover as well.

One man, Daniel Spofford, whose wife was in the first class, was very impressed by Mary's manuscripts. He studied them carefully on his own, and understood enough to do some healing work. When Mary heard of this she invited him to attend her next class free of charge.

Spofford was so moved by this experience that he wrote to his teacher during the course: "Many, many times each day I ask myself, do we students realize what is held out for our possession?" He felt the difference between Mary's writing and teaching was like the difference between "the printed page of a musical score compared to its interpretation by a master." He hoped he was worthy to give back to her a little of what she had given to him.

Teaching students was like raising a family — Mary found her work was never done. While some pupils left her class and became successful healers, others found the discipline too hard and turned against their teacher. Wallace Wright, the son of a Universalist minister, came to class full of questions. At the end, he told a fellow classmate, Ellen Locke, that the last lesson was worth the price of the whole course.

DANIEL SPOFFORD

Wright left New England to practice what he had learned from Mary in Knoxville, Tennessee, where another of her students was located. At first he had good success. Then he got into a quarrel with the other student. He started to rebel against the strict self discipline needed for the healing work. He began to have doubts about what he was trying to do and lost his ability to heal. In anger he wrote to his teacher demanding his tuition money back and two hundred dollars extra in compensation.

She refused, telling him, "To be happy and useful

67

is in your power, and the science I have taught you enables you to be this, and to do great good to the world."

Returning to Lynn, Wright again demanded a refund and the extra two hundred dollars. When Mary still said no, he wrote a letter to the *Lynn Transcript*, saying that Moral Science was nothing more than mesmerism. He wanted to stop anyone else from taking her course.

When Wright called Mary's teaching mesmerism, he meant to discredit her, trying to link her ideas with a form of hypnotism in which one person yields his thoughts to another. Franz Anton Mesmer, a German physician, first brought this practice to public notice in Vienna in 1775.

Mary was quick to respond to Wright. Mesmerism, where one belief drives out another, originates with man, not with God, she maintained. Moral Science "enables us to determine good from evil, and to destroy the latter by understanding first, what is error and what truth…undertaking this great work 'in the name of Almighty God.'"

Wright fought back. Some of Mary's other students rose to her defense. So much excitement was aroused by the controversy in the *Lynn Transcript*, that it was hard to buy a paper the next day. Mary put up a strong front, but she told her old friend, Mrs. Ellis, that she felt the mental anguish of such a debate.

Although Wright did not succeed in stopping Mary's classes, his arguments pushed her to make an important change. In the past Mary had allowed her students to rub their patients' heads while praying for them. Now she saw how this practice led to confusion. It prevented her students from full reliance upon God as the only healing power. She told them to stop depending on physical methods, and turn wholly to God.

How could Mary strengthen her students so that they could rely on prayer alone? Opening her Bible one day, she found this passage: "Now go, write it before them...and note it in a book." Perhaps if she wrote down her ideas more clearly, that would help. Following this leading, she decided to give up her teaching for the time being, and in 1872 concentrated all her energies on writing a book.

One of her young students, George Barry of Lynn, was like a son to her. He ran errands, found Mary places to stay, worked on her finances, and above all, copied and recopied her manuscript. In 1873 Mary submitted her book to a publisher. It was rejected with such severe criticism that she felt she had to revise the whole thing. After many more months she tried again. Again, she was refused. The publishers "could not understand it, and would not attempt to print it."

Mary did not give up. She continued to revise her book to make the meaning clearer. She found a new title for it, *Science and Health*. Some months later one of her students, Dorcas Rawson, brought Mary a copy of the Wycliffe Bible. John Wycliffe was a religious reformer in England who had been persecuted by the church for translating the Latin Vulgate Bible into English. He had used the words "science and health," where the later King James version uses, "knowledge of salvation" (Luke 1:77). How amazed Mary was to find the title of her book embedded in the Bible all along!

JOHN WYCLIFFE
1324-1384

69

Wycliffe had glimpsed the link between science (knowledge of God) and health, (wholeness) five hundred years earlier.

Mary also realized that the term Christian Science rather than Moral Science more accurately described her subject. "I named it *Christian*," she explained, "because it is compassionate, helpful and spiritual."

As Mary wrote, "Such a flood tide of truth was lifted upon me at times it was overwhelming, and I have drawn quick breath as my pen flew on..."

When the author next felt ready to present her work to the public, she talked things over with her students. Some of them agreed to subscribe to a fund, and a printer, W. F. Brown of Boston, was found. Mary had to pay all the costs and supervise the work; in effect, she was self-publishing the book. She explained what this meant to her student, Putney Bancroft.

"After two years and a half incessant labor seven days in a week, I have now the part of proof reader to

Mary's home at 8 Broad Street, Lynn, Mass.

take or my book will be spoiled and go over again the 400 pages correcting it because they have made the plates from proofs in which they made many blunders. I have now to count the letters of every word I take out or insert when I make corrections. Tired to death, broken down with persecutions, no home to rest in, invalids all around me, one room only etc, etc., to work in."

Finally in the spring of 1875, Mary had a breakthrough. Looking out from her boarding room window, she found that the house across the way, 8 Broad Street, was for sale. She bought it for $5,650.00. Most of the rooms had to be let out to tenants to help pay the mortgage, but she kept the front parlor and a tiny attic room for herself. This was sparsely furnished with a bed, bureau, table, one straight-backed chair and a rocking chair with a horsehair seat. Straw matting, like tatami, covered the floor. The room was not comfortable — like an oven in summer, an icebox in winter — but at least it was all hers. She could stand on a chair by the single skylight in the sloping roof, and look out at the city of Lynn, or lie on her cot and look up at the stars, when the day's work was done. Here she finished her book.

Still there were delays in its printing. Brown, the printer, made changes in the copy as he went along, altering the meaning, which Mary had to correct. She, also, made further revisions, which slowed him down. At one point, with no explanation, Brown stopped work altogether. Even though Mary had paid him seven hundred dollars, nothing she said could get him to continue. She was disgusted.

Months passed. Mary could not get rid of a persistent feeling that her last chapter should include something about the nature of evil. She was reluctant to do this, but at the same time felt "the divine purpose that this should be done... Accordingly, I set to work, contrary to my inclination, to fulfill this painful task..." She inserted a history of what she saw as wrong mental practice, or malpractice.

Although she did not know it, the printer resumed his work at the same time. The afternoon he set out from Boston to Lynn, Mary set out from Lynn to Boston. They met at the Lynn train station and were both surprised: Mary to learn that the printer had finished his work and come for more copy; Brown to find her on her way to Boston with the closing chapter of the book. No word had passed between them.

In spite of these setbacks, Putney Bancroft had never known his teacher so continuously happy in her work. "Although she was writing, teaching and preaching, and occasionally treating some severe case beyond a student's ability to reach, her physical and mental vigor seemed to be augmented rather than depleted."

Finally, in October 1875, a thousand copies of *Science and Health* came off the press. It had been nine years since Mary started making notes on the Bible, following her fall on the ice. She had copyrighted *The Science of Man* in 1870. Its ideas were

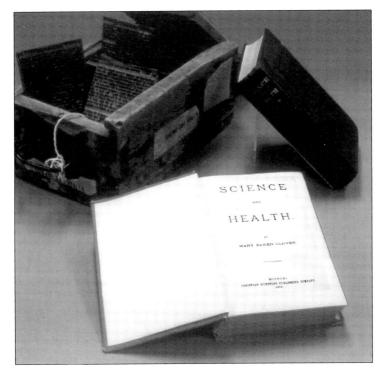

First edition of Science and Health, *published in 1875, with printing plates in box*

so new, it offered such an original basis for health, and the subject was so unfamiliar, she knew the merits of Christian Science had to be proved before a work could be profitably published.

Now, after countless healings — George Norton, James Ingham, Alanson Wentworth to name a few — she was ready to put her thoughts before the public.

"This book is indeed wholly original, but it will never be read," wrote one reviewer. "The book is certainly original and contains much that will do good," countered another. Neither writer could know that *Science and Health with Key to the Scriptures*, as it was later called, would go through more than five hundred printings in Mary's lifetime.

So many people were healed just from reading her book, that in later editions Mary included a section

A. BRONSON ALCOTT

"I have come to comfort you."

called "Fruitage." This last chapter of *Science and Health*, a hundred pages long, overflows with letters of gratitude for all kinds of healings: not only physical ills such as tuberculosis, rheumatism, cataracts, heart disease, broken bones, cancer, and so on; but also for changes in character, for spiritual awakening and uplift.

Mary sent copies of her work to influential thinkers of the day, most of whom never responded. Bronson Alcott, a philosopher and friend of Ralph Waldo Emerson, and father to the well-known author of *Little Women*, wrote back: "Accept my thanks for your remarkable volume entitled 'Science and Health' which I have read with profound interest..." When churchmen ridiculed her book from the pulpit and in the press, Alcott went to see Mary in Lynn. His first words were, "I have come to comfort you."

—⚡—

From the time she was little and gave away her clothes, Mary had wanted to help others. She opposed religious beliefs which taught that only some people were saved while the rest were damned, even though it meant defying her father. Her own life was a testing ground for what she taught. She had lost her dearest brother, her husband, her mother, and her son — all those closest to her — but that only strengthened her reliance on God, and deepened her sympathy for others. She passed through many years of sickness and poverty, scorn and misery, before winning her way to health and a clear idea of her spiritual purpose. That purpose she had sensed when she was eight and heard her name called three times. She had been afraid then, not sure what the voice meant. Later she wrote in a poem:

> "I will listen for Thy voice,
>   Lest my footsteps stray;
> I will follow and rejoice
>   All the rugged way."

By her careful listening, Mary discovered what she called the Science that underlies the record of healing in the Bible. Jesus had shown the way, and proved the power. His understanding of God was the key. Did Mary get it right? She left that up to the public with this tender assurance:

"You can prove for yourself, dear reader, the Science of healing, and so ascertain if the author has given you the correct interpretation of Scripture."

"The divine Principle of healing is proved in the personal experience of any sincere seeker of Truth."

(*Science and Health*, page 547:6; Preface x:22)

What Happened Next?

ASA GILBERT EDDY

To the surprise of her friends, on New Year's Day, 1877, Mary married one of her students, Asa Gilbert Eddy. He was a kind, gentle man, who gave up his successful practice as a healer when he married his teacher. Gilbert was devoted to Mary and did everything in his power to help her, from researching copyright laws to cleaning house.

Two years later George Glover came east to visit his mother. It was the first time they had met in twenty-three years. George, a United States Marshal of the Territory of Dakota, wore high boots, a big hat, and had a big, black moustache. His voice was loud and commanding.

Mother and son tried to get along, but their interests were totally different. George wanted to get gold out of the ground; Mary was seeking her "treasure in heaven." George was impressed by Mary's healing power but did not understand her teaching. City life cramped him, his family out west needed him home, and he left after a rather unsatisfactory three-month visit.

That same year, 1879, Mary and nine of her students had voted to form a Christian Science church in Boston, based on her discovery of how Jesus healed people. A few months later the members asked her to be their pastor. One of them wrote, "While Mrs. Eddy, [Mary] the eloquent, earnest, pleader for her infant Cause, was the chief object of interest, it was the gentle, yet evidently strong nature of Asa Gilbert Eddy, which formed a necessary 'background,' and seemed to make the meetings altogether complete."

Gilbert was such a strong supporter that Mary felt desolate when her faithful husband died in 1882, after only five years of marriage. She poured out to her friends, "...he was *strong, noble,* the *one true heart* that has been so much to me... I never shall master this point of missing him all the time...but I can try, and am trying as I must..."

"Dear Son," she wrote to George, could he come and stay with her? But George was too tied up with gold mining and his own family. He replied he could not leave home.

But there were many others who were eager to leave home and see Mary. In 1884, a young woman in Nebraska, Lulu Blackman, feared she would be an invalid for the rest of her life. A friend from Chicago came on a visit and told her about a new method of healing. Lulu was taken to Chicago to receive treatment from one of Mary's students, and was healed through Christian Science. Reading *Science and Health* and longing to understand it clearly, she felt

Glover family portrait circa 1887.
Left to right: Mary, George
Washington Glover II (Georgy),
his wife Harriet Ellen Bessant
(Nellie), Evelyn and Gershom

she must meet the author. She wrote asking admission to Mary's class, stating, "If it is necessary for me to be a dissatisfied and miserable Christian, I am not ready for this instruction, for I am, and always have been, a very happy one."

Mary's response was a simple, "Come and see."

When George came in 1887, bringing Nellie, his wife, and their three children, the timing could not have been worse for his mother. Since her son's last visit, Mary had opened a college for her classes, published several pamphlets, (which later became books), revised *Science and Health*, and launched the *Journal of Christian Science*, a bimonthly magazine. Keeping the *Journal* going with articles, poems, notices, answers to questions, and fillers was a full-time job, without dealing with the constant stream of visitors and students swirling around her. "Was so full of calls and perplexing questions last week, I about lost my head," she told a student.

Mary was in the middle of a series of classes when George and his family arrived. It was still a marvel to George that the mother he had known — so loving, yet so weak and sickly — was now healing and teaching many students. He asked if Nellie, his wife, could join one of her classes. "If [your wife] will read to me a page of Science and Health *wherever I open to it*, I will then talk with you about her joining my next class," Mary replied. She was more concerned that Nellie (and George) learn to read fluently first, and that their children be educated. Mary was won over by her grandchildren. She took them onto the platform where she was preaching one Sunday to introduce them to the congregation.

All George wanted was a "regular" mother, someone who cooked and cleaned and kept house. He did not understand Mary's writing, editing, and publishing. He resented the trusted place her students had in her household, which made him feel left out. After six months he took Nellie and the children back home to Lead, South Dakota. Mary sent him money for his gold prospecting, and had a fine, five-bedroom house built for the family in Lead, but she could not be his idea of a mother.

Gold pin of prospector's tools given by George to his mother, 1910.

The year following George's visit, Mary made a series of unusual moves. She left Boston for Concord, New Hampshire. Then within six months, she disorganized everything she had taken such pains to build. She dissolved the students' association, shut down her college, disorganized the church, and told the current editor of the *Journal* not to consult her about its contents. Why?

There was too much rivalry and infighting among the students, who thought about themselves more than they thought of others. Mary also sensed too much emphasis on her personality. She wanted the young folk to "do some thinking for themselves and the cause without my aid."

—ᴡᴡ—

When she re-established the church in 1892, it had a new form of government, and was called The Mother Church, or The First Church of Christ, Scientist. It served as a link for all the "branch" churches that had sprung up in different parts of the country. As the church developed, Mary saw the need for a set of rules, which later grew into the *Manual of The Mother Church*. These rules were "impelled by a power not one's own," Mary explained, "were written at different dates and as the occasion required." Their main thrust was to give church members a model, a rule of law, above the grasp of personal control. The *Manual* evolved just as *Science and Health* had done, put to the test of time and circumstance. In its final form it was a slim volume, only 138 pages long, and it still governs the church.

In 1906, the New York *World* newspaper sent one of its reporters, James Slaght, to South Dakota to persuade Mary's son, George, that his mother was unable to run her own affairs, and that her students held her hostage. The ploy was to convince him to act on

Mary's behalf and "free" her from her students. George was intensely loyal to Mary, but he had a suspicion that her household screened her from him.

Mary had been living quietly, absorbed in her work for the church and her movement. She did not encourage visitors or the press. Her one break was a daily drive around the streets of Concord. Journalists, looking for something sensational to report, made up all kinds of stories about her. On Sunday, October 28, 1906, the New York *World* ran the headline:

Original Mother Church shortly after completion in 1894

MRS. MARY BAKER G. EDDY DYING

FOOTMAN AND "DUMMY" CONTROL HER

Tricked by false reports, both George and his daughter agreed to file suit, in Mary's name, against her closest students. Although the originators of the suit pretended it was for Mary's benefit, it really was an attempt to discredit her and her teaching, and gain control of her money.

In consideration of Mary's age, the court did not ask her to come before them, but appointed three experts — a judge, a lawyer and an alienist (a psychiatrist) — to interview her in her home and test her mental competency. She answered their questions with such directness and clarity that the opposing lawyer told one of his juniors, "She's smarter than a steel trap." The suit collapsed in August 1907, six months after it started. Later, Mary settled $245,000 on her son,

George, and he promised not to contest her will.

In January 1908, Mary left her much loved home in Concord and moved to Boston. A month later she received a resolution that reads in part:

> BE IT RESOLVED, THAT THE CITY OF CONCORD, THROUGH ITS BOARD OF ALDERMEN AND COMMON COUNCIL, IN JOINT CONVENTION, CONVEY TO MRS. EDDY,
>
> 1. ITS APPRECIATION OF HER LIFE IN ITS MIDST,
> 2. ITS REGRETS OVER HER DEPARTURE, AND
> 3. THE HOPE THAT THOUGH ABSENT SHE WILL ALWAYS CHERISH A LOVING REGARD FOR THE CITY, NEAR WHICH SHE WAS BORN, AND FOR ITS PEOPLE, AMONG WHOM SHE HAS LIVED FOR SO MANY YEARS."

Mary did cherish a loving regard for the people of Concord, and showed it in practical ways. For several years while she lived there, she paid a shoe store to provide shoes for all the schoolchildren who needed them.

Her bookkeeper of many years, Calvin Frye, wrote in 1902, "I know that she gives away a large sum in private charities. These gifts have in some years amounted to $80,000."

"To love and to be loved, one must do good to others," was what Mary lived by. This prompted her to make yet another bold move. On August 10, 1908, she wrote to the trustees of the Christian Science Publishing Society which she had founded:

> "Beloved Students:
> It is my request that you start a daily newspaper at once, and call it the Christian Science Monitor. Let there be no delay. The Cause demands that it be issued now…"

THE CHRISTIAN SCIENCE MONITOR

STOCK EDITION.   BOSTON, MASS., WEDNESDAY, NOVEMBER 25, 1908.—VOL. I., NO. 1.   PRICE TWO CENTS.

CARNEGIE DOES NOT WANT TO BE TARIFF WITNESS

Steel Magnate Says He Has Served His Time in Matters and Views Are Well Known.

71 YEARS OLD TODAY

Chairman Payne of Ways and Means Committee Makes Public Correspondence With Multi-Millionaire.

SHIP RELIEF IS SAFE AT LUZON

CALL TROOPS TO QUELL STUDENTS

CONSTRUCTION WORK RAPIDLY PROGRESSES ON GREAT DAM ACROSS THE CHARLES RIVER BASIN

Lock and Sluices Completed and Machinery Installed in New Lock-House on Boston Side of Stream.

LOCK IN OPERATION

CITY WINS $5000 IN LAND CASE

Judgment Is Entered in Case of Property Purchased From Cemetery Trustee and Superintendent.

BOSTON LIBRARY IS GIVEN A RARE BOOK COLLECTION

Mrs. Louise Chandler Moulton and Philip Bourke Marston Volumes Include Many Autograph Copies.

NO DEMOCRACY, ZUEBLIN SAYS

37,000 TURKEYS FOR HOME MARKET

ASK INJUNCTION AGAINST CHELSEA SHOE WORKERS

Walton V. Logan Alleges Union Men Interfered With Employes at Factory After Strike Was Declared.

NAMES EIGHT MEN

FIREMAN SAVES ENTIRE FAMILY

Brave Rescuer Swung From Roof 70 Feet Above Sidewalk in New York to Aid Seven Persons.

SAVES CHILDREN AND WIFE AT FIRE

BROCKTON CHURCH DEDICATION NEAR

SPEAKER'S CLUB FOR HARVARD MEN

UNVEIL STATUE OF GEN. SHERIDAN AT WASHINGTON

Salute of 17 Guns Fired in Honor of Civil War Hero When Son Pulls Aside Covering of Memorial.

NOTED MEN PRESENT

NIGHT SCHOOLS FOR DES MOINES

Success of Plan Last Year Causes Educational Board to Resume Sessions This Season.

GOV. GUILD MAKES GOETTING ADVISER

NEW FACTORY SOON TO START

THANKSGIVING DAY FORECAST

EXPERT REVIEWS CONDITIONS IN THE DISTURBED BALKAN COUNTRIES

Interesting Phase of Economic Duel Between England and Germany Discussed.

LANDMARK HISTORY

Installment Stories of Situation in Near-Far East Presented for Readers of The Christian Science Monitor.

SARDINIA BEACHED BECAUSE OF FIRE

Liner Burned Just Outside Malta While on Her Way From Liverpool—Many Lives Lost.

LOCKS AND SLUICES IN CHARLES RIVER DAM.

The Christian Science Monitor, *front page of first edition, November 25, 1908*

In a little over a hundred days from the time of this letter, the newspaper rolled off the presses. November 25, 1908, was dark and foggy, but to Mary it was the lightest of all days.

Members of Mary's household, composite photograph circa 1910

"This is the day our daily paper goes forth to lighten mankind," she told the workers in her household. "The object of the *Monitor* is to injure no man, but to bless all mankind."

In its career since then, the *Monitor* has often been praised for its objective journalism. It has won many awards, including several Pulitzer prizes — an interesting twist since Joseph Pulitzer, newspaper mogul, was one of Mary's harshest critics, and an instigator of the lawsuit in 1907.

When the *Monitor* came out in 1908, the Christian Science movement, which had started with just one

*Mary addressing
a crowd from
her balcony in
Concord, N.H.,
June 1903*

student in 1867, now numbered many thousands. Churches had sprung up not only all over the United States, but also in Canada, Great Britain, Germany, France, the Netherlands, South Africa, and Australia. Christian Science Societies — budding churches — could be found in such diverse cities as Buenos Aires, Geneva, Manila, Nassau, and Hong Kong.

Mary had become a national figure, yet she still thought of herself as a student of the Science she discovered. "I long for less to do as a leader and more time to be a student," she wrote to a Protestant minister. She was often asked, "Who will be your successor?" In reply she did not single out a person or a group of people, but answered, "What remains to

lead on the centuries…is man in the image and like-
ness of the Father-Mother God."

—◊—

In December 1910, in her ninetieth year and after
a brief illness, Mary passed peacefully away in her own
home. Her last written words were, "God is my life."

1821   *July 16*   Mary Morse Baker born in Bow, New Hampshire, the youngest of six children.

1843   *December 10*   Marries George Washington Glover "Wash." They move to Charleston, South Carolina.

1844   *June 27*   Wash Glover dies, age 34. Mary returns home to New Hampshire.
September 12   Georgy, Mary's son, born.

1851   *May*   Son Georgy sent to live with the Cheneys in North Groton, New Hampshire.

1853   *June 21*   Marries Dr. Daniel Patterson, dentist and homeopathist.

1866   *February 1*   Falls on ice in Lynn, Massachusetts, and is not expected to live.
February 4   Recovers from injury by turning to God in prayer.
March   Daniel deserts Mary, who is left homeless and penniless..

1870   *August*   Teaches her first class in Lynn, Massachusetts.

1872   *February*   Begins writing her book, *Science and Health*.

1873   *November*   Divorces Daniel Patterson on grounds of desertion.

1875   *October 30*   *Science and Health* published, 1000 copies printed.

1877   *January 1*   Marries Asa Gilbert Eddy.

1879   *April*   Students vote to form Church of Christ, Scientist.

1882	*June 2*	Husband Gilbert Eddy dies.
1883	*April*	Publishes first issue of *Journal of Christian Science*.
1889	*December*	Formally disorganizes church.
1892	*September*	The Mother Church, The First Church of Christ, Scientist organized.
1898	*November*	Teaches her last class in Concord, New Hampshire.
1908	*November*	First issue of *The Christian Science Monitor* is published.
1910	*November*	Works on final revision of *Science and Health with Key to the Scriptures*.
1910	*December 1*	Last written words, "God is my life."
	December 3	Dies peacefully at home in Chestnut Hill, Massachusetts

FURTHER READING

To find out more about Mary Baker Eddy, look for these books at your library, bookstore, or on the internet:

Eddy, Mary Baker. *Science and Health with Key to the Scriptures*
(Boston, Mass.: The First Church of Christ, Scientist, published continuously since 1910)
The book Mary wrote after discovering how Jesus healed people. Her lifework which she continued to revise and refine for more than thirty years.

Retrospection and Introspection
(Boston, Mass.: The First Church of Christ, Scientist, published continuously since 1891)
Mary's autobiography.

Gill, Gillian. *Mary Baker Eddy.* Radcliffe Biography Series
(Reading, Mass.: Perseus Books, 1998)
The most complete one volume work on this subject. The emphasis is on Mary's life struggle, seen through the eyes of the current women's movement. Like an attorney, Gill sifts through the evidence presented by previous biographers both for and against Mary, and in most cases, comes out strongly in her defense. Gill writes with vigor, intelligence, passion, humor. Part of the book is so dramatically presented, it feels like a play.

Nenneman, Richard A. *Persistent Pilgrim: The Life of Mary Baker Eddy*
(Etna, New Hampshire: Nebbadoon Press, 1997)
Nenneman read more than ten thousand letters written by Mary! The strongest impression he gained was of her loneliness and persistence. His book has many interesting quotes, also background information on Christian Science, Puritanism and hypnotism.

Parsons, Cynthia. *The Discoverer: Mary Baker Eddy*
(Chester, Vermont: Vermont Schoolhouse Press, 2000)
> Parsons, longtime educator and author, has written specifically for middle
> school readers. Because its publication date coincided with the writing of
> *Come and See,* I have not yet read this book, but want you to know of
> its availability.

Peel, Robert. *Mary Baker Eddy: The Years of Discovery*
Mary Baker Eddy: The Years of Trial
Mary Baker Eddy: The Years of Authority
(New York, N.Y.: Holt, Rinehart and Winston, 1966, 1971, 1977)
> This three volume set is excellent for reference. Peel is a scholar who
> can keep many trends of thought going at once, like a chess player or
> a juggler. He shows the pattern of ideas in nineteenth century religion,
> medicine and science while telling the complex story of Mary's life. He
> interviewed people who knew Mary, and writes with penetration and
> insight.

Smaus, Jewel Spangler. *Mary Baker Eddy: The Golden Days*
(Boston, Mass.: The Christian Science Publishing Society, 1966)
> Written for young people. Smaus complements Peel by filling in the homey
> details, such as how the Baker children got on together, and what they had
> for Thanksgiving dinner. After writing this book, Smaus continued her
> research, checking on Georgy's Civil War record, for example, and inter-
> viewing his son. Her fascinating series, entitled "Family," was published by
> Longyear Museum, Chestnut Hill, Massachusetts, in their *Quarterly News.*

You might also like to check the website:
www.marybakereddy.org

A

Alcott, A. Bronson, 74
Anderson, Major, 41-42

B

Baker, Abigail Ambrose (mother) (Mrs. Mark Baker), 2-4, 6-7, 12-14, 15, 21, 22-23, 28-29
Baker, Abigail (sister) (Mrs. Alexander Tilton), 4, 7-8, 15-16, 27, 29-30, 36, 40, 53, 54, 60
Baker, Albert (brother), 4, 8-9, 17-18
Baker, George (brother), 4, 14, 17-18, 20-21, 25, 29, 48
Baker, Hannah Lovewell (great-grandmother), 5-6
Baker, James (uncle), 10
Baker, Mark (father), 9, 10-12, 15, 20, 21, 26, 29, 30, 33, 48
Baker, Martha (sister) (Mrs. Pilsbury), 4, 7-8, 15, 34, 39, 40, 48, 59
Baker, Mary. See Eddy, Mary Baker
Baker, Mrs. (grandmother), 2, 4-6, 15
Baker, Samuel (brother), 4, 14, 19, 45
Bancroft, Putney, 70, 72
Barry, George, 69
Bessant, Harriet Ellen "Nellie" (daughter-in-law) (Mrs. Georgy Glover), 78, 79
The Bible, 3-4, 9, 11, 22, 34, 38, 43, 50-51, 52, 55-56, 57-58, 61, 62, 69 72, 75

Blackman, Lulu, 77-78
Boston, Massachusetts, 83
Bow, New Hampshire, 6-9
Brown, Rebecca and Arietta, 50
Bubier, Samuel and Mrs., 49
Bull Run, Virginia, 44

C

Camp Randall, Madison, Wisconsin, 43
Charleston, South Carolina, 19-25, 41-42
Charleston *Mercury* (newspaper), 19-20
Cheney, Mahala (Mahala Sanborn, Mrs. Russell Cheney), 26, 30-31, 34-36
Cheney, Russell, 30-31, 34-36, 44
Christian Science, 68, 70, 73, 77, 85, 86
The Christian Science Monitor (newspaper), 83-86
Christian Science Publishing Society, 83
Civil War, 41-45, 47-48
Clark, Rev., 50, 51
Clement, Sarah, 28
Concord, New Hampshire, 6, 79, 81, 83
Congregational Church, Bow, 10, 11
Corinth, Mississippi, 47-48
Corser, Rev. Enoch, 16
Covenanters, 4
Cowper, William, 24
Crafts, Hiram and Mary, 57-58, 59, 60-61
Cushing, Dr., 49-50, 51

D

Dartmouth College, 8
Dresser, Julius, 52

E

East Stoughton, Massachusetts, 57-58,
    60-64
Eddy, Asa Gilbert (third husband), 76, 77
Eddy, Mary Baker (Mrs. George
    Washington Glover, Mrs. Daniel
    Patterson)
  childhood of, 2-18
  as healer, 38, 47, 50-51, 54-60, 62,
    72-74
  illness of, 12-13, 26, 32, 37,
    45-46, 49-50
  marriages of, 21-22, 32-33, 76
  as pastor, 77, 79, 80
  as publisher, 70-71, 78, 83-85
  as teacher, 27-28, 57-58, 61, 65-69,
    72, 78
  as writer, 22, 29, 37, 42, 53, 56,
    69-72, 75, 78-79, 80
Eighth Wisconsin Infantry Eagle
    Regiment, 42-43, 47-48
Ellis, Mrs. and Fred, 56
Evening Courier (newspaper), 46

F

The First Church of Christ, Scientist,
    77, 80, 86
The Floral Wreath (magazine), 22
Fort Sumter, South Carolina, 41-42
Freemasons, 22, 25
"Fruitage," 74
Frye, Calvin, 83

G

The Gaults (Bow neighbors), 7, 14, 17
Glover, Eliza Ann (sister-in-law)
    (Mrs. Samuel Baker), 14
Glover, Georgy (son)
    (George Washington Glover II),
    26, 28-31, 33-36, 42-44, 47-48,
    53, 64, 76-77, 78, 79, 80-83
Glover, Major George Washington
    "Wash" (first husband), 14-15, 16,
    19-25, 53, 64
Glover, Mrs. See Eddy, Mary Baker
The Glovers (in-laws), 30-31
God, 4, 11, 12, 14, 46, 52, 54,
    55-56, 59, 61, 65-66, 68, 70,
    75, 86

H

Haiti, 21, 24-25
Hall, David, 44
Healings, 12-13, 38, 50-51, 54-55,
    58-60, 62, 73, 74
Hillsborough, New Hampshire, 8-9
Hoke, Michael, 22
Homeopathy, 38-39, 49
Hunter, Martha, 46
Hypnotism, 45-47, 59, 68

I

"I'm Sitting Alone" (poem), 53
The Independent Democrat
    (newspaper), 42
Ingham, James, 58-59

J

Jesus, 46, 50, 56, 75, 77
Journal of Christian Science
    (magazine), 78-79, 80

The Science of Man (book), 66
Scotland, 4
Scott, William, 63
Slaght, James, 80
Slavery, 23-24, 25
Smith, Marcia, 37
Smith, Myra, 37, 40, 41
Spiritualism, 57, 58, 59
Spofford, Daniel, 66-67
Swampscott, Massachusetts, 56

T

Taunton, Massachusetts, 58, 60
Tilton, Albert (nephew) (Abi's son),
     28-29
Tilton, Alexander (brother-in-law),
     15-16
Tilton, New Hampshire. See Sanbornton
     Bridge
Truth, 50, 56, 61, 66, 68, 70, 75

W

Wallace, Sir William, 4-5
Washington, 17, 42, 44, 47
Wentworth, Alanson and Sally, 62-63
Wentworth, Charles, 63
Wentworth, Lucy, 62-64
W.F. Brown printery, Boston, 70-71, 72
Wheet, Joseph and Charles, 39-40
White Mountains, New Hampshire, 21
Wilmington, North Carolina, 21, 24-25
Winona, Minnesota, 36
Wright, Wallace, 67-68
Wycliffe, John, 69-70

—w—

ABOUT THE AUTHOR

Isabel Ferguson has a degree in history from Edinburgh University, and a graduate degree in education from Boston University. She first learned about Christian Science as a child growing up in China during the second World War, and has since spent many years in its full-time healing practice. This biography, bringing together her love of writing and the exploration of spiritual ideas, has been a joyful adventure. The author and her husband live in Massachusetts. Their family includes three grown sons, a daughter-in-law and two grandchildren.

—w—

ABOUT THE ILLUSTRATOR

Joan Wolcott graduated from the Rhode Island School of Design with a degree in graphic design. Her interests in book design, drawing, and children came together a few years ago when she illustrated and designed her first children's book, *Who Dropped Down the Chimney?* written by Isabel Ferguson. Her work also includes tutoring children part-time. She lives in Massachusetts with her husband and their son.